Sharp WRITING

Related Titles

Sharp Math
Sharp Vocab
Sharp Grammar

sharp
WRITING

Building Better Writing Skills

PUBLISHING

New York

This publication is designed to provide accurate and authoritative information in regard to the subject matter covered. It is sold with the understanding that the publisher is not engaged in rendering legal, accounting, or other profesional service. If legal advice or other expert assistance is required, the services of a competent professional should be sought.

Kaplan Publishing books are available at special quantity discounts to use for sales promotions, employee premiums, or educational purposes. Please email our Special Sales Department to order or for more information at kaplanpublishing@kaplan.com, or write to Kaplan Publishing, 1 Liberty Plaza, 24th Floor, New York, NY 10006.

Contents

Introduction

Dear Reader,

Are your business e-mails so long that they're often ignored? Are there words you frequently misspell? Do you misuse *they're, there,* and *their*?

Whatever the reason, you picked up this book, which means you want to improve your writing—a smart decision. Why? **Because knowing and using proper writing will get you places**—on standardized tests, in the workplace, and in everyday life.

Since elementary school, you've been learning the parts of speech, parts of sentences, and their uses. Yet many well-educated, successful people retain little of what they learned. You need look no further than local street and shop signs, newspapers, and the Internet for evidence of this problem.

The goal of this book is to present the principles of great writing one last time, using a unique **Building Block Method** that helps you retain the information. You don't need to commit every bit of information in this book to memory. What you take away is the knowledge of what makes good writing and how you currently measure up.

The experts at Kaplan devised this teacher-approved method to make learning as painless as possible. You'll begin with the basic rules of writing. Then you'll move on to application of those rules in real-life writing formats, and you'll develop your own **Writing Guide** to keep track of errors you make frequently. When you are aware of your weaknesses, you can find and correct mistakes more easily, and you'll know how to proceed.

There's no smarter way to learn. So get started—good writing is only a few building blocks away!

HOW TO USE THIS BOOK

The chapters in this book are divided into three sections, beginning with sentence fundamentals, so everything else builds upon a firm foundation.

Section I: Sharper Writing

Here you'll cover the fundamentals of grammar, usage, style, punctuation, and spelling.

Section II: Sharper Writing Stages

This part will develop your prewriting, writing, and editing skills.

Section III: Sharper Writing Formats

Straightforward templates for the most common types of writing.

Whether you read this book from start to finish or only want to brush up on certain topics, this book will help you to systematically improve your skills. Each chapter contains five key components:

1. Building Block Quiz

Begin each chapter with a short quiz. The first few questions cover material from earlier lessons; if you get them wrong, go back and review! Other questions will test your knowledge of the material to be covered in that chapter, targeting the information you need to focus on. You'll get even more review from explanations that tell you why each choice is right or wrong.

2. Detailed Lessons

Each chapter explains one specific topic in detail, with lots of relevant examples and strategies to help you remember what you need to know.

3. Plentiful Practice

Repetition is the key to mastery. Be prepared to practice, practice, practice! You'll find everything from simple matching exercises to exercises that ask you to apply the skills you're learning to practical, real-life situations. By "learning from all sides," you're much more likely to retain the information.

The answers follow the Summary and precede the Chapter Quiz.

4. Summary

Each chapter concludes with a concise review of key points.

5. Chapter Quiz

At the end of each chapter, you'll take a quiz covering material in that chapter and key concepts from previous chapters, to practice what you've learned and assess your progress.

Writing Guide

Throughout the book, you will be prompted to create your own Writing Guide (similar to style sheets used by professional editors)—a unique document on which you note all your problem areas. Anything you come across in this book that you respond to by saying, "I didn't know that," or "I have trouble with that," should be included. We've added prompts for some, called **Sharp Writing Tips**, to jumpstart an entry for you rather than be used verbatim.

You may wish to keep your guide in a blank notebook or on your word processor, with sheets headed:

- Parts of Speech
- Grammar, Mechanics, Punctuation
- Prewriting
- Writing
- Editing
- Business Writing
- Personal Correspondence and
- Academic Writing.

To promote even greater retention, we suggest you organize and type your final Writing Guide.

With a system as easy as this, good writing is well within your reach. All you have to do is take the first step. Good luck!

SECTION I
Sharper Writing

The Parts of Speech and Their Uses

Start your study of grammar with this 10-question Building Block Quiz.

BUILDING BLOCK QUIZ

Read each sentence below carefully. Determine the part of speech of the underlined word or phrases.

1. Ramon needs a new <u>car</u>.

    (A) noun functioning as a subject

    (B) present tense verb

    (C) noun functioning as an object

    (D) verbal functioning as an adjective

    (E) object of the preposition

2. He <u>went</u> to the used car dealership on Saturday.

    (A) intransitive verb

    (B) past tense verb

    (C) participle functioning as an adjective

    (D) adverb describing the verb

    (E) present perfect tense verb

3. The dealer showed him a <u>silver</u> sedan.

    (A) object of the preposition

    (B) gerund functioning as an adverb

    (C) coordinating conjunction

    (D) noun functioning as an adjective

    (E) descriptive adjective

4. The color was not exactly what <u>he</u> had in mind.

    (A) future perfect tense verb

    (B) pronoun functioning as the subject

    (C) limiting adjective

    (D) noun functioning as the subject

    (E) pronoun replacing the noun *Ramon*

5. Ramon told the dealer he would <u>definitely</u> buy the sedan if it was red.

    (A) infinitive functioning as an adverb

    (B) correlating conjunction

    (C) adverb modifying *buy*

    (D) adverb modifying *he would*

    (E) noun functioning as an object of the preposition

6. "We just sold a red one yesterday, <u>but</u> I think I know where I can get another one" said the dealer.

    (A) participle functioning as an adverb

    (B) coordinating conjunction

    (C) adjective modifying the noun *yesterday*

    (D) subordinating conjunction

    (E) preposition that shows the relationship between *sold* and *know*

7. "Perfect," said Ramon; "that would be <u>great</u>."

    (A) subordinating conjunction

    (B) adverb modifying the verb *be*

    (C) adjective modifying the adjective *perfect*

    (D) adjective modifying the demonstrative pronoun *that*

    (E) verbal functioning as an adjective

8. The dealer made some phone calls, and located a red sedan a few miles <u>away</u>.

    (A) preposition showing the relationship between *few miles* and *located*

    (B) adjective modifying the noun *miles*

    (C) noun

    (D) adverb modifying the verb *located*

    (E) past tense verb expressing an action of the dealer

9. He told Ramon it would be ready <u>between two and three o'clock</u> on Monday.

    (A) clause functioning as a correlating conjunction

    (B) adjectival phrase describing the adjective *ready*

    (C) adverbial phrase telling when it *would be*

    (D) prepositional phrase functioning as an adverb

    (E) noun phrase used as a pronoun

10. "That's perfect," said Ramon <u>excitedly</u>.

    (A) adverb describing the car

    (B) adjective describing the noun *Ramon*

    (C) gerund functioning as an adverb

    (D) superlative adjective

    (E) adverb describing the verb *said*

BUILDING BLOCK ANSWERS AND EXPLANATIONS

1. C Nouns are people, places, or things. *Car* is a thing, and it is the object of the verb *needs*.

2. B Verbs express action or a state of being. *Went*, the past tense of *go*, is an action.

3. E Adjectives modify or describe nouns or pronouns. *Silver* describes the noun *sedan*.

4. E Pronouns most often replace nouns or other pronouns. *He* replaces the noun *Ramon*; it is not the subject of the sentence (*the color* is).

5. C Adverbs modify or describe verbs, adjectives, and other adverbs. *Definitely* modifies the verb *buy*, telling us how Ramon would make the purchase.

6. B Conjunctions connect words or parts of sentences. *But* connects the independent clauses *We just sold a red one yesterday* and *I think I know where I can get another one*, showing the relationship between those two clauses. That makes it a coordinating conjunction.

7. D *Great* describes the pronoun *that*, making it an adjective.

8. D *Away* describes the verb *located*; it answers the question "where?" Therefore, it is an adverb.

9. D *Between* is a preposition, so *between two and three o'clock* is a prepositional phrase. It functions as an adverb, telling "when" the car would be *ready* (adjective).

10. E *Excitedly's* –*ly* ending is a clue that it is probably an adverb; its function as a modifier of the verb *said* (past tense of *say*) confirms it. Gerunds end in –*ing*.

The parts of speech work together. Verbs, adjectives, and nouns have little meaning by themselves. Instead, they function within sentences to convey meaning. And words can act as different parts of speech depending on how they are used in a sentence.

The word *show* can be a noun, as in "The show is about to begin." But it can also be an adjective, as in "show time," or a verb, as in "show me the way to go home." To determine the part of speech, determine how the word is used in the sentence.

NOUNS

> **WRITING SPEAK**
>
> A noun is a person, place, or thing.

Types of Nouns

- Singular, as in pencil, mouse, or book, or **plural,** as in pencils, mice, or books
- **Collective** or **group**, naming a single entity composed of more than one part, such as jury, class, or team
- **Concrete**, naming things that can be directly experienced by the senses: igloo, sandwich, phone; or **abstract**, naming an idea, concept, or quality that can't be experienced by the senses: fairness, truth, neurosis
- **Proper**, naming *specific* people, places, or things: Maria Callas, University of Pennsylvania, White House; or **common**, naming *general* people, places, or things: opera singer, school, building

In the following sentences, the nouns are underlined:

We are going to the game.

The concert is being held in Memorial Auditorium.

This application requires an additional essay.

Jeanne's cooking class is meeting on Saturdays through June.

Recently, our State Legislature passed a law governing the licensing of hair stylists.

Nouns can be subjects: who or what the sentence is about—the person, place, or thing that performs the action (or state of being). Examples above include *we, concert*, and *legislature*. Nouns may also be objects: words that receive the action of the verb. Examples above include *essay*, and *law*. The noun *hair* and the possessive *Jeanne's* are nouns functioning as adjectives.

Practice 1

Underline each noun in the paragraph below and identify whether each is **singular** or **plural**, **concrete** or **abstract**, **proper** or **common**.

> When grilling steaks, allow the charcoal to heat up until it is coated with ash. If the coals are not hot enough, the steaks will not sear properly. Chef Robert Lamouille of the Shoreline Steakhouses recommends this test: if you hear a sizzle when the steaks touch the grill, you know the coals are right. After just two or three minutes, turn the steaks over. If a flare-up occurs, spray the flames with water, or move the steaks to another part of the grill. Remove from the heat after another two minutes, and allow the steaks to rest for five minutes before slicing.

When a noun functions as a subject, it can be *single* (one subject) or *compound* (two or more subjects). Single subjects may be singular or plural, but there is only one of them in a sentence. Here are examples of single subjects:

> The *bushes* around her house are overgrown.
>
> Liam's tennis *racket* needs to be restrung.
>
> Our local auto repair *shop* does good work.

Compound subjects are made up of two or more distinct subjects, connected by the word *and, or,* or *nor*. Here are some examples of compound subjects:

> *Tim and Juanita* are working on the science project together.
>
> Either *the farmers* or the *developers* will have control of the land.
>
> *Vice President Jacobus and her department* are going on a retreat.

PRONOUNS

WRITING SPEAK

Pronouns usually take the place of or refer back to one or more nouns or pronouns; they can also take the place of whole phrases or clauses. The word or words replaced are called the **antecedent**.

Dr. Liu is on vacation; Dr. Liu is in Hawaii.

Dr. Liu is on vacation; *he* is in Hawaii.

The Human Resources and Accounting Departments are hiring.

They are hiring.

A **phrase** is a set of words that are grammatically linked but do not include both a subject and verb.

The people who waited on line got their tickets first.

They got their tickets first.

I found *my mother's favorite dessert* in the pie store.

I found it in the pie store.

A **clause** is a set of words that are grammatically linked and include both a subject and a verb. If a clause can stand alone as a sentence, it is **independent**.

The class is studying.

A clause that cannot stand alone is **dependent**.

When we begin studying

Pronouns can take the place of either type of clause. For example:

Will *one of the people who finished eating* clean the table?

Will *somebody* clean the table?

Types of Pronouns

Personal:	*Singular subject:* I, you, she, he
	Singular object: me, her, him *Plural subject:* we, you, they *Plural object:* us, them
Reflexive:	*Singular:* myself, yourself, himself, herself, itself *Plural:* ourselves, yourselves, themselves **Correct:** I gave myself permission to sleep late. **Incorrect:** He's going to the game with herself.
Relative:	*Subject; refers to people:* who *Object; refers to people:* whom *Refers to objects:* which *Usually refers to objects:* that etc. **Correct:** The dog who is dirty needs a bath. **Incorrect:** Our soccer team, whom no one can beat, won the trophy.
Demonstrative:	this, that, these, those
Indefinite:	Singular: another, anybody, anyone, anything, each, either, everybody, everyone, everything, little, much, neither, nobody, no one, nothing, one, other, some-body, someone, something Plural: both, few, many, others, several
	Singular or Plural: all, any, more, most, none, some

> **SHARP WRITING TIP**
>
> Words like *everybody* and *everyone* are singular.

After Jeremy completes his exam, *he* will be graded.

The pronoun *he* refers to *Jeremy*. Since *Jeremy* names one male, the pronoun is also singular and male:

Incorrect: Clarice and Larissa went the party after *she* finished work.

Correct: Clarice and Larissa went to the party after *they* finished work.

> **REMEMBER THIS!**
>
> A pronoun must refer to a clear and unique antecedent and agree with it in number and gender.

Some pronouns are **subjects** (I, you, he, she, we, they, who) and others are **objects** (me, him, her, us, them, whom). Remember, objects receive the action of the sentence, while subjects perform it. If you're not sure whether to use *I* or *me, he* or *him, we* or *us, or who* or *whom,* you need to understand the difference between subjects and objects. Let's look at an example:

Shandra called Mark.

Shandra, the subject of the sentence (the person who performs the action of *calling*), can be replaced by the subjective pronoun *she* or *who* (you wouldn't say *Her* called Mark). *Mark* is the object, the person who receives the action of calling, so his name can be replaced by the objective pronoun *him* or *whom.*

Practice 2

Circle the correct pronoun(s) in each of the sentences below.

1. Neither Bill nor (I/me) caused the damage.

2. He gave the assignment to Janice, (who/which) had to skip class due to illness.

3. When Congress is in session, (it/they) decide(s) on many important matters that affect our country.

VERBS

> **WRITING SPEAK**
>
> A verb expresses actions, events, or states of being.

Verbs, by their tenses, also ground the sentence in time. They can be a single word, a compound, or a phrase formed by adding one or more helping verbs (such as *will, shall, may, might, can, could, must, ought to, should, would, used to,* and *need*) to the main verb.

Basic Verb Tenses

Tense	Definition	Example
Present:	indicates that something is happening now.	She *mows* the lawn.
Past:	indicates that something happened in the past.	She *mowed* the lawn.
Future:	formed with the helping verb *will* or *shall*; indicates that something has not happened yet.	She *will mow* the lawn.
Present Perfect:	formed with the helping verb *have* or *has*; indicates that an action was completed at an unspecified point in the past, but is still true.	She *has mowed* the lawn.
Past Perfect:	formed with the helping verb *had*; indicates an action took place at a specified point in the past.	She *had mowed* the lawn
Future Perfect:	formed with the helping verbs *will have* or *shall have*; indicates that an action will have occurred at a special point in the future.	She *will have mowed* the lawn by the time her allowance is due.

In the following sentences, the verbs are underlined:

The Green Bay Packers <u>are</u> my favorite football team.

The Packers <u>will be</u> the next Super Bowl champions.

My team <u>would have had</u> an excellent record last season, but injuries <u>sidelined</u> many of our best players.

Transitive and Intransitive Verbs

In the sections on nouns and pronouns, you saw that those parts of speech could function as objects. When a sentence has an object, its verb is called *transitive*. That means the action of the verb is transferred to something else (the object).

The professor assigned a term paper.

Raul gave plenty of reasons to doubt him.

Assigned and *gave* are **transitive** verbs because they need objects (in this case, *a term paper,* and *plenty of reasons*). You wouldn't say, "The professor assigned," or "Raul gave"; an object is needed to show what the action refers to. Verbs that do not need objects are **intransitive**.

> The dog barked loudly.
>
> Genie complained when she got her grades back.

Barked and *complained* need no object; they are *intransitive*.

Verbals

Remember learning that nouns can function as subjects, adjectives, adverbs, and objects? Verbs can perform a similar variety of functions within a sentence. Verbals are formed from verbs, but by themselves are not verbs. They include gerunds, participles, and infinitives.

Gerunds always end in *–ing* and act as nouns (which may be subjects or objects).

> *Running* is my favorite sport. (*Running* is the subject)

Participles can be present (ending in *–ing*) or past (ending usually in *–ed*), and function as adjectives.

> The *smiling* baby caught everyone's attention.
>
> The *damaged* section of the wall had to be replaced.

Participles can also function as part of the verb. Present and past forms both use the help *verb to be*. Here are examples of the present participle and past participle used as verbs:

> The baby *is smiling*.
>
> The wall *was damaged*.

Infinitives are the base forms of verbs preceded by the word *to*. They can function as nouns within sentences (meaning of course that they can function as subjects, adjective, adverbs, and objects). For example:

> *To drive* with the top down is one of my favorite ways to enjoy the nice weather.

Infinitives can also be part of the verb:

> My boss asked me *to write* a memo to our department.

Practice 3

For the following sentences, indicate whether the underlined verb is
(a) **transitive**, (b) **intransitive**, or (c) **helping**.

4. Ridding your computer of viruses <u>can</u> be complicated.

5. First, you should <u>install</u> anti-virus software.

6. Use software that eliminates viruses rather than just identifying
   them.

Circle the correct tense for each sentence below.

7. We (had eaten / had ate) all the popcorn before the movie even
   started.

8. The car (teared / tore / torn) around the corner.

9. The fog (creeped / crept) in and (was blanketing / blanketed)
   the shore in mist.

ADJECTIVES

> **WRITING SPEAK**
>
> **Adjectives** describe or modify nouns and pronouns. They tell us
> which one, what kind, or how many.

Descriptive or **qualifying** adjectives express a quality of the nouns they
modify. They answer questions such as *what kind, what color, what size,*
and *what shape.*

The <u>fast</u> roller coaster was Gray's favorite.

Why can't that radio station play anything but <u>Top 40</u> music?

Limiting adjectives answer questions such as *how many, how much,
which one,* and *whose.* They can take the form of an article (a, an, the),
refer to a quantity (one, sixty, first, several, many), or indicate possession
(my, theirs, whose).

It's <u>my</u> book.

We go on vacation the <u>second</u> week of January.

<u>The</u> alarm is going off.

Practice 4

In each sentence that follows, underline adjectives (if any) and identify what each modifies.

10. I just finished a drivers' education course.

11. My test will be at the Division of Motor Vehicles on Tuesday.

12. Before I can drive, I need insurance.

ADVERBS

> **WRITING SPEAK**
>
> **Adverbs** describe, modify, or limit verbs, adjectives, and other adverbs.

Adverbs tell us *when; where; how; why; under what conditions; and to what degree* something happened. They differ from adjectives, which tell us about the thing (or person or place) itself.

Recognizing Adverbs

Most adverbs end with the suffix *–ly*, making them easy to identify.

We walked through the hospital *quietly*.

That customer complained *angrily* about the delay.

The adverb *quietly* describes how we walked; *angrily* describes how the customer complained.

A few adverbs don't end in *–ly*.

Rafael slept *late*.   Rafael slept *here*.

The adverb *late* tells when Rafael slept, and *here* tells where.

And not all words ending in *–ly* are adverbs. Some adjectives also end with the suffix:

A *friendly* woman lives next door.   The flowers were *lovely*!

The adjective *friendly* describes the noun *woman*, and *lovely* describes the noun *flowers*.

Adjective-Adverb Confusion

Adjectives and adverbs are often misused for each other. To avoid making this error, identify the part of speech that is being modified.

The rapid transit train left the station quickly.

Rapid and *transit* modify the noun train, therefore they are adjectives. *Quickly* explains how the train left, making it an adverb.

Speak softly and carry a big stick.

Softly explains how you should perform the action of speaking. It is an adverb. *Big* describes the noun *stick*, making it an adjective.

Comparative and Superlative Forms

Adjectives and adverbs also vary in degree. When comparing two things, we use the **comparative** degree, and when comparing three or more things, we use the **superlative.** The comparative is usually followed by the word *than* and is formed with the suffix *–er* or the word *more*, as in *Gordon is smarter than Tom* or *This road is more direct than the other.* The superlative is formed with the suffix *–est* or the words *most* or *least*, as in *Shireen is the smartest engineer* or *This road is the most dangerous.*

Adjective	Comparative	Superlative
interesting	more interesting	most interesting
large	larger	largest
happily	more happily	most happily
funny	funnier	funniest

A few adjectives and adverbs have irregular comparative and superlative forms. They include *good* (better, best), *bad* (worse, worst), *far* (further, furthest), *little* (less, least), and *much* (more, most).

Adjectives and adverbs that are absolute should never appear in the comparative or superlative form. Something is either *unique* or it sn't; it can't be *more unique* than something else. Other words in this category are: *complete, entire, fatal, ideal, impossible, preferable,* and *whole.*

> **SHARP WRITING TIP**
>
> Not all adjectives can be put into comparative and superlative forms.

Practice 5

Find and underline each adverb. Then identify the word it modifies, and label it a verb, adjective, or adverb.

13. I came up with a way to easily remember my friends' birthdays.

14. I used to remember them early and forget to send a card, almost miss them, or remember them late.

15. You don't need to buy a fancy birthday book to accurately acknowledge important dates.

Fill in the blank in the following sentences.

16. Adjectives modify _____.

17. a. *Good* is an _____.

    b. *Badly* is an _____.

18. Use the comparative form to compare _____ things.

19. Use the superlative form to compare _____ things.

20. Modifiers should be placed _____.

PREPOSITIONS

WRITING SPEAK

Prepositions are words that show a relationship between one or more nouns or pronouns and one or more other words in a sentence.

Prepositions often express a time or spatial relationship between the words they link. The meaning of a preposition may be difficult to express in words; it is easier to use gestures instead.

Common prepositions:

about	behind	for	off	to
above	below	from	on	toward
across	beneath	in	onto	under
after	beside	inside	out	until
against	between	into	outside	up
along	by	like	over	upon
among	despite	near	since	with
at	during	next	through	within
before	except	of	throughout	without

Prepositional Phrases

Prepositions always appear in **phrases** that begin with a preposition.

> Lean the rakes *against* the shed.

Against the shed is a prepositional phrase showing the relationship between the verb *lean* and *shed*. The phrase answers the question *where*, so it functions as an adverb.

> The firefighters scaled the building *despite the intense heat and darting flames.*

Despite shows the relationship between *the intense heat and darting flames* and *scaled*. Since it modifies the verb, it is an adverb. In the following sentences the preposition is underlined and the phrase is italicized:

> <u>After</u> *the lecture*, I copied my notes <u>*into*</u> *my notebook.*

> Shari's house is <u>*on*</u> *Baker Street*, which you can get to <u>*by*</u> *turning left* <u>*at*</u> *the light.*

> Tia had to decide *between* going to the mall and studying for an exam.

> It was hard to choose <u>*among*</u> the three contestants.

> **REMEMBER THIS!**
>
> *Between* refers to two things. *Among* refers to more than two things.

Common Preposition Pairs

To be idiomatically correct, prepositions are often paired with certain nouns, verbs, and adjectives. Here are some of the more problematic pairings.

approval of	live at (an address)
aware of	live on (a street)
belief in	live in (a city or house)
capable of	need for
compare to (emphasizing likeness)	participation in
compare with (emphasizing difference)	reason for
concern for confusion about desire for	respect for
differ from (a thing)	similar to
differ with (a person)	success in
familiar with	understanding of
interested in	

Practice 6

Underline the prepositional phrase or phrases in the following sentences and decide whether each functions as a noun, adjective, or adverb.

21. Approval of the project won't take place today.

22. When are your neighbors leaving for their vacation?

23. The children were afraid of the scary witch in the movie.

CONJUNCTIONS

> **WRITING SPEAK**
>
> **Conjunctions** join two or more parts of sentences—words, phrases, or clauses—expressing a relationship between them.

Types of Conjunctions

Coordinating conjunctions are words that connect words, phrases, and clauses that are grammatically equivalent. There are seven common coordinating conjunctions: *and, or, nor, for, but, so,* and *yet.* In the examples below, the coordinating conjunctions are underlined:

We are tired <u>but</u> happy.

He got home early <u>and</u> went to bed.

Correlating conjunctions are paired words or phrases used to connect grammatically equivalent elements. The most common are: *as...as, either... or, neither...nor, not only...but also, both...and, not...but, whether...or.*

You must <u>either</u> drive to the bank <u>or</u> complete the transaction online.

<u>Not</u> <u>only</u> is tennis my favorite sport; it's <u>also</u> the one I'm best at.

Subordinating conjunctions introduce dependent clauses (those that can't stand alone as a sentence).

Now that he is eighteen, he can register to vote.

The sentence contains two clauses, *Now that he is eighteen,* and *he can register to vote.* The second is independent; the first is dependent, since *Now that he is eighteen* cannot stand alone. The phrase *now that* establishes the relationship between the clauses.

Here are more examples of subordinating conjunctions.

after	except	since	when
although	how	so that	whenever
as	if	that	where
as if	in order to	though	wherever
because	once	unless	whether
before	rather than	until	while
even though			

REMEMBER THIS!

The same words that function as subordinating conjunctions may also function as prepositions or adverbs.

Practice 7

Circle **T** for true or **F** for false for each of the following statements.

24. **T   F** Correlating conjunctions can join a verb phrase and an adjective.

25. **T   F** Subordinating conjunctions are located at the beginning of independent clauses.

26. **T   F** *Not only* and *but also* are examples of a coordinating conjunction pair.

Circle the correct conjunction type for each underlined word.

27. <u>Even though</u> we lost the game, our team played well.

    (Coordinating, correlating, subordinating)

28. He ordered a large sandwich <u>and</u> french fries.

    (Coordinating, correlating, subordinating)

29. The job interview was <u>both</u> an exciting experience <u>and</u> a nerve-wracking one.

    (Coordinating, correlating, subordinating)

WHAT IT'S ALL ABOUT: THE SUBJECT

The <u>subject</u> of a sentence is *who* or *what* the sentence is about. You can usually find the subject by asking who or what carries out the action of the sentence:

<u>I</u> love to paint.	*Who* loves to paint? *I* do.
On Wednesdays and Fridays, <u>Pearl</u> and <u>Jasmine</u> attend karate class.	*Who* attends karate class? *Pearl* and *Jasmine*.
<u>Absolute power</u> corrupts absolutely.	*What* corrupts absolutely? Absolute power.
<u>Remaining silent</u> can be destructive.	*What* can be just as destructive? *Remaining silent.*

As you can see, the subject usually comes before the verb (what the subject is or does or has done to it). Most of the time, subject-verb is the word order we expect in the English sentence, the rhythm of our language. There are three exceptions:

- when writers invert the order for effect
- when sentences begin with *there is/are, it is/they are* or *was/were*
- questions

Understood Subjects

Do your homework!

Who or what does the homework? The subject is *understood* to be *you*. This is an **imperative** sentence—it gives advice or issues a command.

Kinds of Subjects

The **simple** subject is the subject minus any modifiers or articles (*a/an, the*). The **complete** subject is the subject with its modifiers and articles:

Simple: The old yellow <u>house</u> on Turner Road is being demolished tomorrow.

Complete: <u>The old yellow house on Turner Road</u> is being demolished tomorrow.

The simple subject can be a single word, a phrase (a group of words without a subject and verb), or a clause (a group of words containing both a subject and verb):

One word: There's a <u>rabbit</u> in your hat.

Phrase: <u>The phrase "once in a blue moon"</u> means every two and a half years.

Clause: <u>What you just said</u> was the best thing anyone has ever said to me.

These subjects are still simple (even though there's more than one word).

The **predicate** of a sentence is the verb and anything that logically belongs with it—the objects, modifiers, or complements (we'll define these shortly). The predicate usually ends the English sentence. In the sentences below, complete subjects are underlined and predicates are in brackets:

<u>I</u> [love to paint.]

<u>Pearl and Jasmine</u> [attend karate class on Wednesdays and Fridays.]

<u>Remaining silent</u> [can be just as destructive as telling a lie.]

> **WRITING SPEAK**
>
> The **subject** is who or what the sentence is about about (who or what performs or recieves the action). The **predicate** is the verb and any objects, complements, or modifiers.

Predicates can be single or compound. A compound predicate has the same subject for two or more different verbs:

Single predicate:

A <u>good neighbor</u> [helps when asked].

Compound predicate:

A <u>good neighbor</u> [helps when asked] and [asks for help].

Predicates and Sentence Patterns

As you've seen, the basic English sentence pattern is subject-predicate. Predicates come in different shapes and sizes, forming four main sentence patterns:

s-v:	subject–verb
s-lv-c:	subject–inking verb–complement
s-v-o:	subject–verb–direct object
s-v-io-o:	subject–verb–indirect object–object

Linking Verbs and Complements

In some sentences, the base verb is a **linking verb (lv)**—a verb that links a **subject (s)** to its **complement (c)**.

> **GRAMMAR SPEAK**
>
> A **complement** is the part of a predicate that describes or renames the subject. To *complement* means to make perfect or complete; a complement completes the subject. Complements are connected to the subject by a **linking verb.**

I / am / a painter.

s / lv /   c

"Once in a blue moon" / means / about once every two and a half years.

      s   lv   c

The complement *a painter* describes the subject *I*. The phrase *about once every two and a half years* defines *once in a blue moon*.

Forms of the verb *to be* (*am, is, are, was, were, being,* and *been*) often serve as helping verbs, but when *to be* is the base verb (as in the first example) it is a linking verb. Descriptive verbs, such as *become, feel, appear, look, seem, taste, sound,* and *smell*, are often linking verbs as well.

To test for a linking verb, remove the verb and insert an equal sign; does it make sense?

I = painter

Once in a blue moon = about once every two and a half years

This *doesn't* work for predicates that do *not* have subject complements:

Absolute power *corrupts* absolutely.   I *understand* your message.

Absolute power ≠ absolutely.   I ≠ your message.

SHARP WRITING TIP

A verb is a **linking verb** if you can replace it with an = .

Receiving the Action: Direct Objects

While linking verbs connect a subject and complement, **transitive verbs** **(tv)** take their action out on a **direct object (o)**: a person or thing in the predicate. There are a number of types of object; when we simply say "object" we mean the direct object.

I / understand / your message.

s   tv   o

In this sentence, *message* receives the action of the verb; it is what is being understood.

I / will pick up / some milk on the way home from work.

s   tv   o   [prepositional phrases]

Like subjects, direct objects are never in prepositional phrases.

Who It's For: Indirect Objects

The direct object *directly* receives the action of the verb. The **indirect object (io)** *receives the direct object.*

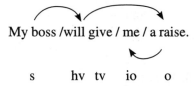

My boss /will give / me / a raise.

s   hv tv io   o

A raise is what will be given, so it is the direct object. But who will receive that raise? *Me*—the indirect object.

Here's one more example:

The police / questioned / Anna about the accident.

     s   tv   o [prepositional phrase]

The police / asked / Anna / many questions about the accident.

     s   tv   io   o [prepositional phrase]

In the first sentence, there is no indirect object; Anna directly receives the action of the verb *questioned*. In the second sentence, *questions* is the direct object and *Anna* the indirect object.

Pattern Variations

As you've seen, the four basic sentence patterns—**s-v, s-lv-c, s-v-o,** and **s-v-io-o**—can vary (1) when writers invert order for effect, (2) in questions, and (3) in *there is/are* constructions:

[Why] did / you / give / Michaela / credit [for my work]?
[adv] hv / s / v /   io   / o [prepositional phrase]

TYPES OF SENTENCES

Sentence type is determined by the number and type of clauses a sentence contains. Before attacking them, quickly review what a subordinate clause is. A subordinate clause cannot stand alone. It is *subordinate* to an independent clause, without which it doesn't express a complete thought.

Subordinate clauses usually begin with a **subordinating conjunction** or a **relative pronoun**. In the following examples each clause is bracketed with a slash between subject and predicate, and the subordinate clause indicator (the conjunction or relative pronoun) is in bold.

[You / act] [**as if** you / don't care].
[independent clause] [subordinate clause]

[[**Whoever** / finds my wallet] / will get a reward.]
[[subordinate clause within] independent clause]

Note that in the second example, the subordinate clause is the subject of the sentence.

Type 1: The Simple Sentence

A simple sentence contains one independent clause and no subordinate clauses. The subject and predicate can be single or compound, but the sentence contains only *one* subject-predicate pair.

I / must be true to myself.   Then I / can be true to others.
S   V   S   V

Type 2: The Compound Sentence

A compound sentence contains two or more independent clauses and no subordinate clauses. The two independent clauses are connected by a **coordinating conjunction** or by a semicolon with or without a **conjunctive adverb** (see chapter 1):

[You / must be true to yourself]; otherwise, [you / cannot be true to others.]

[independent clause] ; conjunctive adverb [independent clause]

Type 3: The Complex Sentence

A complex sentence contains one independent clause with one or more subordinate clauses.

[Before you can be true to [those you / love]], [you / must be true to yourself.]

[subordinate clause [subordinate clause]], [independent clause]

Type 4: The Compound-Complex Sentence

A compound-complex sentence consists of two or more independent clauses and one or more subordinate clauses.

[I / know that [if I / am not true to myself]], [I / cannot be true to others.]
[independent clause [subordinate clause]], [independent clause]

Practice 8

In each of the following, identify subject (s), verb (v), and object (o) and then the sentence type.

30. Every road has two directions.

31. Those who sleep with dogs will rise with fleas.

32. Under a ragged coat lies wisdom.

33. Since we cannot get what we like, let us like what we can get.

SUMMARY

The parts of speech are the foundation of smarter writing. They are the components of phrases, clauses, and sentences. When you are confident in your knowledge of the parts of speech and their forms and uses, your writing will improve. Here is an overview of what you've learned.

A **sentence** is a group of words containing both a **subject** and a **predicate** and expressing a **complete thought**. The **subject** is who or what the sentence is about. In **imperative sentences**, the subject is understood to be *you*. Subjects are never in prepositional phrases. The **predicate** is the verb with its objects, modifiers, and complements.

Both subjects and predicates can be **single** (one singular or plural subject or predicate) or **compound** (two or more singular or plural subjects or predicates).

The basic order for English sentences is subject-predicate, but that order is reversed in questions, *there is/are* statements, and sentences that are inverted for effect. There are four common subject-predicate patterns: **s-lv-c, s-v-o, s-v-io-o,** and **s-v.**

A **clause** is a group of words containing a subject and predicate. Clauses may be **subordinate** or **independent**. There are four types of sentences: **simple** (one independent clause), **compound** (two independent clauses), **complex** (one independent clause and one or more subordinate clauses), and **compound-complex** (two or more independent clauses and one or more subordinate clauses).

PRACTICE ANSWERS AND EXPLANATIONS

Practice 1

Steaks (plural, concrete, common), charcoal (singular, concrete, common), ash (singular, concrete, common), coals (plural, concrete, common), steaks, chef (singular, concrete, common), Robert Lamouille (singular, concrete, proper), Shoreline Steakhouses (plural, concrete, proper), sizzle (singular, abstract, common), steaks, grill (singular, concrete, common), minutes (plural, abstract, common), steaks, flare-up (singular, concrete, common), flames (plural, concrete, common), water (singular, concrete, common), steaks, part (singular, concrete, common), grill, heat (singular, concrete, common), minutes, steaks, minutes.

Practice 2

1. **I.** *I* is part of the compound subject of the sentence; if it read "The damage was done by neither Bill nor _____" the answer would be *me* because it is an object.

2. **Who.** The antecedent is "Janice." The pronoun *which* refers to objects, and *who* refers to people. Note that the pronoun *who* introduces the clause *(who had to skip class due to illness)* that modifies *Janice*.

3. **It.** Congress, the pronoun's antecedent, is a collective noun, so it calls for a singular pronoun.

Practice 3

4. **c**   (the main verb is *be*)

5. **a**   (*anti-virus software* is the object)

6. **a**   (*software* is the object)

7. *had eaten.* This action was already completed before the time of another action (the movie starting).

8. *tore.* The past tense form of the irregular verb *tear* is *tore*.

9. *crept, blanketed.* Both verbs should be in the simple past tense as they occured at the same time. *Crept* is the past tense form of *creep*.

Practice 4

10. Adjectives *drivers'* and *education* both modify the noun *course*.

11. Possessive pronoun *my* acts as an adjective limiting the noun *test*; *motor* describes *vehicles*.

12. No adjectives; if you chose *before*, recall that adjectives don't indicate time–review the section on adverbs.

Practice 5

13. *Easily* is an adverb that tells how the speaker *remembers* (verb).

14. *Early* also tells how the speaker *remembers* (note that it can also function as an adjective, as in the *early bird*); *almost* modifies the verb *miss; late* describes the verb *remember.*

15. *Accurately* modifies the verb *acknowledge.*

16. nouns and pronouns

17. a. adjective; b. adverb

18. two

19. three or more

20. as close as possible to what they modify.

Practice 6

21. *Approval* is the subject of the sentence, and it is modified by the prepositional phrase *of the project.* That means the phrase functions as an adjective.

22. *For their* vacation is an adverb that modifies the verb *leaving.*

23. *Afraid* is an adjective that describes *the children.* It is modified by the adverbial prepositional phrase *of the scary witch. In the movie* is also a prepositional phrase; it acts as an adjective, describing the noun *witch.*

Practice 7

24. **False.** Correlating conjunctions only join grammatically equal parts of a sentence, such as a noun and a noun, and a verb phrase with a verb phrase.

25. **False.** Subordinating conjunctions are found at the beginning of dependent clauses.

26. **False.** *Not only* and *but also* are correlating conjunctions.

27. **Subordinating.** *Even though* begins a dependent clause, and joins it to the independent clause *our team played well.*

28. **Coordinating.** *And* joins the nouns *large sandwich* and *french fries.*

29. **Correlating.** *Both/and* is a common pair of correlating conjunctions that connects the noun phrases *an exciting experience and a nerve-wracking one.*

Practice 8

30. [Every road / has two directions.]

    [s-v-o]

    Independent clause.

    Simple sentence.

31. [Those [who / sleep with dogs] / will rise with fleas.]

    [s [s-v]—v]

    Subordinate clause within independent clause.

    Complex sentence.

32. [Under a ragged coat lies / wisdom.]

    [v-s]

    Independent clause.

    Simple sentence. (Notice that the sentence structure is inverted.)

33. [Since we / cannot get [what we / like]], [let us / like [what we / can get]].

    [s-v-o [s-v]], [s-v-o [s-v]].

    [Subordinate clause [subordinate clause]], [independent clause [subordinate clause]]

    Complex sentence.

CHAPTER 1 QUIZ

Identify the part of speech of each of the underlined words in the following paragraph. Note the tenses of verbs, and types of conjunctions.

Most people think of sushi as raw fish. In fact, it actually refers to
 1   2
rice. Both popular types of sushi, makizushi and nigirizushi, are
                                                       3
based on rice topped or mixed with seafood and other
  4
ingredients. Makizushi refers to the roll shape created by encasing
                                          5   6   7
the rice and other ingredients in nori, which is rolled into a

8

cylinder in a bamboo mat. Nigirizushi, which was developed in

Tokyo, <u>consists</u> of a pad <u>or</u> ball of rice topped with seafood.

9   10

Read each sentence below carefully and determine the part of speech needed to fill in the blank.

11. Jeffery talked on the phone_____.
12. The quarterback did an excellent job, _____ his team lost anyway.
13. Did you ever see such a _____ play?
14. Kara is missing _____ favorite coat.
15. What an incredible _____!
16. His computer _____ well.
17. Every movie ever made is listed _____ that guidebook.
18. Alexandra could _____ stay on line or go home.
19. When the show was over, they _____.
20. Our grocery store always has the _____ tomatoes.

CHAPTER 1 QUIZ ANSWERS AND EXPLANATIONS

1. *Most* is an adjective—it modifies the noun by answering the question "how many" (in this case, *people*).

2. *Actually* is an adverb because it modifies the verb *refers*.

3. *And* is a conjunction; it joins the nouns *makizushi* and *nigirizushi*.

4. *Based* is a past tense verb that expresses the action of its subjects, *makizushi* and *nigirizushi*.

5. *Roll* is an adjective because it describes the noun *shape*. (Note that *roll* can also be used as a noun and a verb.)

Chapter 1 Quiz Practice Answers and Explanations *(cont'd)*

6. *By* is a preposition that describes the relationship between the noun (*created shape* or *roll*) and the verb *encasing*.

7. *Encasing* is a gerund acting as the object of the preposition *by*.

8. *Nori* is a noun. It would also be correct to note that it functions here as the object of the preposition *in*.

9. *Consists* is a verb—it expresses the state of being of the noun *nigiri-zushi*.

10. *Or* is a (coordinating) conjunction that links the nouns *pad* and *ball*.

11. **Adverb.** The word would tell how Jeffery talked on the phone. (*quietly, incessantly, loudly*).

12. **Conjunction.** A coordinating conjunction—specifically, *but*—would connect these two independent clauses and show the relationship between them.

13. **Adjective.** This word would describe the play (*mysterious, awful, fabulous*).

14. **Adjective.** A possessive pronoun (*your, her*) is needed here.

15. **Noun.** The missing word is described by the adjective *incredible*, so it must be a noun (*store, sandwich, musician*).

16. **Verb.** An action word (*works, functioned, will search*) is needed to tell *what* the computer does or did well.

17. **Preposition.** A preposition (*in, within*) would tell us the relationship between *movie* and *guidebook*.

18. **Conjunction.** A correlating conjunction is needed, specifically the word *either*, which pairs with *or*.

19. **Verb.** An action word or phrase (*clapped, went home, stayed in their seats*) would complete this sentence and tell us what the subject did.

20. **Adjective.** This word would describe the tomatoes (*mushiest, ripest, smallest*).

CHAPTER 2

Structure, Syntax, and Usage

BUILDING BLOCK QUIZ

Determine the part of speech of the underlined words in the following sentences and write your answer below each word.

1. <u>Television</u> news <u>increasingly</u> covers the lives of celebrities.

2. A firewall should be <u>used</u> <u>on</u> your computer to protect it

   from viruses.

3. Let's <u>either</u> go to the airport now, <u>or</u> call Mike

   and tell him we will be <u>late</u>.

Choose the letter that describes the grammatical error in each of the following. If the sentence is correct as written, choose (E).

4. Went to the game on Saturday.
   - (A) dangling modifier
   - (B) sentence fragment
   - (C) passive voice
   - (D) verb tense shift
   - (E) no error

5. You're scarcely eating anything from the buffet; one should at least try the salad bar.

   (A) run-on sentence
   (B) subject-verb agreement
   (C) pronoun shift
   (D) misplaced modifier
   (E) no error

6. Shelly bought a souvenir while on her vacation that cost too much money.

   (A) misplaced modifier
   (B) sentence fragment
   (C) verb tense shift
   (D) subject-verb agreement
   (E) no error

7. Please print fifteen copies of today's lesson plan before coming to class.

   (A) passive voice
   (B) run-on sentence
   (C) pronoun shift
   (D) dangling modifier
   (E) no error

8. That group of businesswomen look like it is heading home.

   (A) subject-verb agreement
   (B) misplaced modifier
   (C) sentence fragment
   (D) passive voice
   (E) no error

9. My favorite radio station played too many commercials, and doesn't play enough good songs anymore.

   (A) run-on sentence

   (B) dangling modifier

   (C) pronoun shift

   (D) verb tense shift

   (E) no error

10. The book was read by Mr. Potter.

   (A) misplaced modifier

   (B) subject-verb agreement

   (C) verb tense shift

   (D) passive voice

   (E) no error

BUILDING BLOCK ANSWERS AND EXPLANATIONS

1. *Television* is a noun that functions as an adjective describing the noun *news*. *Increasingly* is an adverb that modifies the verb *covers*.

2. *Used* is a verb, and *on* is a preposition.

3. *Either* and *or* are correlating conjunctions. *Late* is an adjective that describes the subject *we*.

4. B There is no subject, making this a fragment. To correct it, add a noun, such as, "*Bill* went to the game on Saturday."

5. C The pronouns are inconsistent. The first, *you,* is second person plural; the second, *one*, is impersonal.

6. A Did the souvenir or the vacation cost too much? The modifier *cost too much* is ambiguous. The words should be rearranged to convey the intended meaning clearly: "Shelly bought a souvenir that cost too much while on vacation," or "While on a vacation that cost too much, Shelly bought a souvenir."

BUILDING BLOCK ANSWERS AND EXPLANATIONS *(cont'd)*

7. E   The sentence is correct.

8. A   The noun *group* is singular, even though it is made up of a number of individuals, so it takes a singular verb, *looks*.

9. D   The first time the verb *to play* is used, it is in the past tense *(played)*, but the second is in the present *(play)*—they should both be in the same tense.

10. D   There is no reason to use the passive voice in this sentence. It should be in the active voice: "Mr. Potter read the book."

SUBJECT-VERB AGREEMENT

Chapter 1 reviewed the parts of speech and their functions. This chapter will focus on some of the most common grammatical errors and how to avoid them.

What It Is

This seemingly straightforward rule causes difficulty for many writers: singular subjects take singular verbs, and plural subjects take plural verbs.

   Incorrect: Abe don't like his hair cut too short.

The subject *Abe* is singular, and needs the singular form of the verb, *does*: Abe doesn't like his hair cut too short.

Getting It Right

There are four instances when determining subject-verb agreement can be tricky.

1. **Compound subjects** connected with *and* are plural; those connected with *or* are singular or plural depending on the noun closest to the verb.

   Joan and Mary are going to the gallery.

   Either a fox or some raccoons were responsible for the damage.

Since the plural *raccoons* is closest to the verb, the correct verb is *were*.

> **SHARP WRITING TIP**
>
> For compound subjects joined by *or*, the verb agrees with the closest noun.

2. **Collective nouns** take singular verbs when the group as a whole is intended, but plural when they refer to the individual units.

   The family is united in supporting Marilyn.

   The family are always fighting with each other.

> **FLASHBACK**
>
> As you saw in chapter 1, collective nouns are singular nouns that represent a number of individual parts, such as government and team.

3. **Complex sentences,** in which a subject and verb are separated by one or more phrases or clauses, may make agreement unclear. Eliminate them to decide whether subject and verb agree.

   The bridesmaids, waiting in the vestry for their cue to enter the church, was bored.

Although *church* is the closest noun to the verb, it isn't the subject. Since *bridesmaids* is plural, the correct verb is *were*.

4. **Inverted Sentences,** which reverse the typical subject-verb order, can make agreement difficult to determine.

   Does Lee prefer the Dijon mustard?

   Incorrect: There is sixteen candles on the cake.

The plural noun *candles* takes the plural verb, *are*.

Practice 1

Choose the correct verb or verbs for each sentence.

1. Jason and I (is/are) going shopping on Tuesday.

2. My cookbooks, splattered, torn, and otherwise abused with use, (serves/serve) me well.

3. General Jones always (speaks, speak) loudly to his troops.

4. Here (is/are) the answers I've been looking for.

5. Ahead of the pack (come/comes) last year's marathon winner.

Fill in the blanks or circle the correct word in parentheses in each sentence below.

6. Subject-verb agreement means that subjects and verbs must be the same in _____ and _____.

7. In the present tense, only _____ person (singular / plural) verbs take the base + –s form. All others take the base form.

8. Subjects can be single or _____.

9. Compound subjects joined by *and* need a (singular / plural) verb.

10. Compound subjects joined by *or* or nor should agree with the subject that is _____.

SENTENCE FRAGMENTS AND RUN-ON SENTENCES

What They Are

Sentence fragments are groups of words that are presented as sentences but lacking a subject or a verb, or both, or unable to stand alone as a sentence.

No verb: The well-dressed man

No subject: Walked to school in the rain

Dependent: Because he was in a hurry

In the first fragment, the verb is missing. All we have is a subject. What did the well-dressed man do? In the second fragment, the subject is missing. Who walked in the rain? The final clause is dependent, introduced by the subordinating conjunction because.

Run-on sentences are formed by incorrectly joining two or more independent clauses.

Incorrect: Pick up some milk, don't forget to use the coupon.

This sentence contains two independent clauses (Pick up some milk, and don't forget to use the coupon). Because they can stand alone, they can't be joined with a comma.

Getting It Right

To correct sentence fragments, determine what is missing (subject or verb) and add it or change the parts of speech to convert a word into the missing part. Note that number of words has nothing to do with distinguishing fragments from sentences.

> Taking a taxi when it is raining to keep her shoes from being ruined by the water.

> Taking a taxi when it is raining keeps her shoes from being ruined by the water.

Run-on sentences can be corrected by breaking them into two or more complete sentences, by adding a conjunction (subordinating, coordinating, or correlative), or by changing the punctuation.

> **Incorrect:** When spring break is over, we will get back to work, there will be plenty of studying to do before finals.

The subordinate clause (*when spring break is over*) is correctly attached to the first independent clause (*we are going to get back to work*) with a comma. But the second independent clause, *there will be plenty of studying to do before finals* is joined to the first with only a comma. (See chapter 3 for more information about proper use of commas). A period or semicolon is called for here.

Practice 2

Choose the correct explanation for each of the following sentences or fragments.

11. After the Civil War, and during the antebellum period when many southern homes were rebuilt.

    a. This is a correct sentence.

    b. This is a run on that can be corrected by adding a semicolon after *period*.

    c. This is a fragment that needs both a subject and a verb.

12. The Albrights went to the beach last summer, they said it was the best vacation they ever had.

    a. This is a fragment that can be corrected by adding a comma after *had* and providing the missing information.

    b. This is a correct sentence.

    c. This is a run-on that needs a period, semicolon, or conjunction after *summer*.

13. Dan left Kara returned.

    a. This is a run-on; it can be corrected by adding a comma and a conjunction after *left*.

    b. This is a correct sentence.

    c. This is a fragment that needs a subject and verb.

14. Baseball fans and their knowledge of statistics.

    a. This is a fragment that needs a verb.

    b. This is a correct sentence.

    c. This is a run-on that can be corrected by adding a comma after *fans*.

Part 2

List the three ways to fix a sentence fragment, on your own paper.

Part 3

List the five ways to fix a run-on sentence, on your own paper.

MISUSE OF THE PASSIVE VOICE

What It Is

When a verb is active, the subject of the sentence *performs* an action and an object (if there is one) *receives* the action. In a passive construction, the subject *receives* the action.

Active   The bird ate the birdseed.

Passive   The birdseed was eaten by the bird.

Getting It Right

Note how many more words it takes to communicate the same idea in the passive voice. This is one reason the active voice is preferred for most types of writing. It is more direct and concise.

There are two easy ways to spot passive verbs in your sentences:

1. Does the subject perform or receive the action? Subjects with passive verbs always receive the action.

2. Is there a direct object? Passive verbs never have one.

> **SHARP WRITING TIP**
>
> In most cases, the active voice is preferable.

Practice 3

For each pair, note which sentence is active.

15. a. Turn the key to open the door.

    b. The key is turned to open the door.

16. a. The bank account was closed by Sheila.

    b. Sheila closed the bank account.

17. a. We made vacation plans for spring break.

    b. Vacation plans for spring break were made by us.

There are instances when you should use the passive voice. Choose the passive voice when:

1. You want to deliberately emphasize the receiver of the action instead of the performer

   My fender was dented three times in that parking lot.

2. The performer is unknown

   Mani's wallet was mysteriously returned.

3. You want to avoid mentioning the performer of the action

   The experiment resulted in a new theory.

Practice 4

Is the passive voice used correctly in each of the following sentences?

18. **yes/no**   The clock was adjusted to reflect daylight savings time.

19. **yes/no**   The gift was unwrapped by her.

20. **yes/no**   Shauna and her brother were raised by their grandmother.

Fill in the blanks in the following sentences.

21. Sentences in the _____ voice have a clear agent of action performing the action of the verb.

22. In sentences in the _____ voice, the agent of action is displaced to an object position or removed from the sentence.

23. In general, use the _____ voice whenever possible.

Rewrite each of the following in the active voice on your own paper.

24. The pictures were taken by a professional photographer.

25. Chicken pox was contracted by several children in the class.

For questions 26 and 27, determine which version is most appropriate given the context of the sentence.

26. a. The train has been delayed for hours.

 b. Something has delayed the train for hours.

27. a. Alfonse has requested your opinion.

 b. Your opinion has been requested by Alfonse.

UNNECESSARY SHIFTS

What They Are

Shifts in grammar are movements from one form to another—in verb tenses, pronouns, or the active and passive voices. Shifts can cause confusion, and should only be made if necessary.

Verb tenses are often the only words that place the sentence's action in time. Tense should be used carefully to logically represent the sequence of actions. When tenses shift unnecessarily, your writing becomes confusing.

 Incorrect: If you make a mistake, your grade went down.

The subordinate clause, *if you make a mistake*, refers to something that may happen in the future. But the independent clause is in the past tense. We don't know if the speaker is referring to something that already happened, or something that may happen.

 Correct: If you made a mistake, your grade went down.

Pronouns take the place of nouns, and may be masculine or feminine, singular or plural. Shifting pronoun types within a sentence is another way to confuse your reader.

 Incorrect: If they want to succeed, one should study diligently for tests.

The pronoun *they* is plural, but *one* is singular. The reader must guess at the author's intended meaning.

 Correct: If they want to succed, students should study diligently for tests.

Another type of shift occurs when verbs move from active to passive, or vice versa.

Incorrect: John wrote poetry and many novels were written by him.

The first clause, *John wrote poetry*, is in the active voice. The second, *many novels were written by him*, is needlessly passive.

Correct: John wrote poetry and many novels.

Getting It Right

The key to avoiding verb tense shifts is to be aware of the tense in which you are writing, and to use it consistently.

To correct the previous example, based on the intended meaning, either put the independent clause in the past tense, or the subordinate clause in the future:

Since you made a mistake, your grade went down.

If you make a mistake, your grade will go down.

Correcting shifts in pronouns also requires awareness. If you begin in the third person, don't change to the second in mid-sentence or mid-paragraph. Keep in mind that your goal is to communicate without confusion; say what you mean as clearly as possible.

Incorrect: If one is careful, they can avoid additional cell phone fees.

Correct: If cell phone users are careful, they can avoid additional fees.

SHARP WRITING TIP

Pronoun shifts can cause confusion; avoid moving from second person (you) to third person (he, she, they).

To correct unnecessary shifts between active and passive voice, determine which voice is correct (remembering that the active is almost always preferred), and adjust the incorrect part of the sentence to match it.

Incorrect: Gordon bought the nachos, and they were eaten by the children.

To determine whether the passive voice is needed, ask whether: (1) you want to deliberately emphasize the receiver of the action, or (2) the performer is unknown, or (3) you want to avoid mentioning the performer of the action. Since the example fits none of these situations, the second part of the sentence should be rewritten in the active voice:

Correct: Gordon bought the nachos, and the children ate them.

Practice 5
Avoid or correct the unnecessary shift in each sentence by rewriting the sentence.

28. The museum bought the new painting and _____

    (to display) it prominently.

29. After he drove for hours, the car was stopped by my father at a gas station.

30. She raised her hand and _____ (to answer)

    the professor's question.

31. The governor said he _____ (to campaign)

    for our candidate next year.

32. Because the directions were not listened to, he completed the assignment incorrectly.

MISPLACED, DANGLING, OR AMBIGUOUS MODIFIERS

What They Are
First, let's define the terms: *modifiers* is a general term for descriptive words or phrases, including adjectives and adverbs, prepositional phrases, relative clauses, and others. Be sure it's clear which word or words they describe.

He asked the only girl on a date.

The modifier *only* seems to mean that there is only one girl. But if the author's intended meaning was *he did nothing more than ask the girl on the date*, the modifier should be before the word asked in order to convey the correct meaning.

> By accident, she fell off the ladder onto the ground, which was wobbly.

The *phrase which was wobbly* is a modifier, but what is it modifying? *The ground* was probably not wobbly (no earthquake is mentioned). It probably describes *the ladder*, but is placed too far away from that noun to function properly.

Modifiers are said to *dangle* when they have nothing to modify. They are typically phrases made with participles or gerunds (see chapter 1 for a review of verb forms) that don't relate to the subject or verb in a sentence.

> Waiting at the station, the bus drove by without stopping.

The phrase *waiting at the station* seems to modify the subject, *the bus*. Since the bus is not waiting at the station, the phrase is a dangling modifier. A simple rewrite adds the person intended:

> While Joe was waiting at the station, the bus drove by without stopping.
> Waiting at the station, Joe saw the bus drive by without stopping.

Even when placed next to the term they modify, modifiers can be ambiguous: *Yoko said at the meeting Jake raised a good point.* Did Yoko say it at the meeting or did he raise it at the meeting?

> At the meeting, Yoko said that Jake raised a good point.
> Yoko said that Jake raised a good point at the meeting.

Getting It Right

To keep the meaning of your sentences clear, place modifiers as close as possible to the word(s) they describe. For example, the following two sentences have two very different meanings:

> She almost told her mother all of the details of her trip.
> She told her mother almost all of the details of her trip.

> **SHARP WRITING TIP**
>
> Modifiers should be placed as close as possible to the word(s) they describe.

In the first sentence, *almost* modifies *told*, and in the second, it modifies *all*. If the author intended to say, *she told her mother most, but not all, of the details* the first sentence would be wrong. To fix dangling modifiers, add a word or words to the modifier or the clause to give the modifier something to describe.

By beating the egg whites, the cake will be lighter.

The participle *beating* does not refer to the noun *cake*. An appropriate noun must be added for the sentence to make sense.

By beating the egg whites, you make the cake lighter.

Practice 6

Are the modifiers correctly located in the following sentences? If not, rewrite the sentence correctly.

33. **yes/no**   Hernando gave a present to his mother that was useless.

34. **yes/no**   Considering the economy, my bank account is doing well.

35. **yes/no**   Why don't we meet in front of the black building?

36. **yes/no**   Brooke accidentally spilled coffee on my report that was hot.

37. **yes/no**   Ordering books online, independent bookstores are losing business.

PARALLEL STRUCTURE AND COMPARISONS

What It Is

Matching constructions must be expressed in parallel form. Make sure that when a sentence contains a list or makes a comparison, the items listed or compared are in parallel form.

Getting It Right

Incorrect: I love skipping, jumping, and to play tiddlywinks.

Correct: I love skipping, jumping, and playing tiddlywinks.

Also correct: I love to skip, jump, and play tiddlywinks.

Incorrect: To visualize success is not the same as achieving it.

Correct: Visualizing success is not the same as achieving it.

Word pairs like the following also require parallel form:

Neither...nor	The better [or worse]...the better [or worse]
Either...or	The more [or less]...the more [or less]
Both...and	Not only...but also

Faulty Comparison

Comparisons must do more than be in parallel form. Most faulty comparisons are illogical—you can't compare apples and oranges.

Incorrect: The rules of chess are more complex than checkers.

Correct: The rules of chess are more complex than those of checkers.

Also correct: Chess is more complex than checkers.

Practice 7

Identify any parallel structure problems in the following sentences; think of one way to correct each, then either edit the sentence or rewrite on the line provided.

38. George's hobbies include reading, skiing, and he collects international stamps.

_____

39. The flowers I received from Becker's Florist Shop were fresher but less beautifully arranged than Danson's.

40. It was neither responsible nor did it show proper respect to leave the car blocking the way.

Fill in the blanks in the following sentences.

41. Parallel structure means that two or more items in a sentence have the same _____.

42. In general, parallel structure should be used whenever a sentence has two or more _____ items.

43. Faulty parallelism can be repaired by identifying the parallel items and _____.

Revise the sentences to correct faulty parallelism.

44. At the party, the children stuffed themselves with cake and ice cream and they were exhausted from backyard games.

45. Our foundation serves those who have been displaced because of natural disasters and people needing shelter from relationships that are abusive.

SUMMARY

In this chapter, we covered the most common grammar errors. When you understand them and why they're wrong, you can avoid them in your writing.

Subject-verb agreement means singular subjects take singular verbs, and plural subjects take the plural form of verbs. There are instances when determining subject-verb agreement can be tricky. They include compound subjects, collective subjects, complex sentences, and sentences that begin with *There is, There are, Here is*, and *Here are*.

Sentence fragments and **run-on sentences** are extremes. Fragments don't contain enough information, and run-ons contain too much. Fragments are often missing a subject or verb, so they don't express a complete thought. Run-on sentences are made of at least two independent clauses. In most cases, they either lack a conjunction or proper punctuation that would otherwise link them properly.

Verbs are either in the **active** or **passive voice**. When a verb is active, the subject of the sentence *performs* an action. The active voice places emphasis on the subject, conveys meaning clearly, and is preferred in most types of writing. In a passive construction, the subject *receives* the action. Use of the passive voice can create confusing sentences in which meaning is obscured. It is often used inappropriately, when the active voice is needed.

Shifts are unnecessary moves from one form of a part of speech to another. Shifts of **pronouns, active,** and **passive voice,** and **verb tenses** are the most common. Once you establish whether you are speaking in or referring to first, second, or third person, singular or plural, usage should remain consistent. This follows with active and passive voice, and verb tenses. Tense use should not change unless you are deliberately referring to another time.

Modifiers are words or phrases that describe nouns and verbs. If they're misplaced within a sentence, it's not clear what they're modifying. **Dangling modifiers** are phrases using participles (verbs with *–ing* endings) that have nothing to modify. In other words, they don't relate to the subject or verb of the sentence.

Matching constructions such as items in a list, items being compared, and items connected by coordinating conjunctions, must be expressed in **parallel** form.

PRACTICE ANSWERS AND EXPLANATIONS

Practice 1

1.   Are. *Jason and I* is a compound subject connected by the word *and*, so it takes the plural verb.

2.   Serve. *My cookbooks* is the plural subject, taking the plural verb *serve*.

3.   Speaks. The subject is the singular *General Jones*.

4.   Are. The plural subject is *answers*.

5.   Comes. The singular subject, *last year's marathon winner* follows the verb.

6.   number (singular or plural) and person (first, second, or third)

7.   third, singular

8.   compound

9.   plural

10. closest to the verb

Practice 2

11.   c.   This fragment is a subordinate clause that should be joined with an independent one (a clause that has a subject and verb) to make a sentence.

12.   c.   There are two independent clauses, which must be properly joined.

13.   a.   *Dan left* and *Kara returned* are both independent clauses. They can be divided by a comma followed by *and* or *but*.

14.   a.   The fragment is a noun clause; what do the *baseball fans and their knowledge* do, or what action do they receive? A verb is needed.

Three ways to fix a sentence fragment:

- Attach the clause or phrase to an independent clause.
- Add the missing elements to make a phrase a complete sentence.
- Delete the subordinating conjunction or relative pronoun to make the clause independent.

PRACTICE ANSWERS AND EXPLANATIONS *(cont'd)*

Five ways to fix a run-on sentence

- Turn the clauses into two sentences; separate them with a period.
- Separate the clauses with a comma and the appropriate coordinating conjunction.
- If the clauses are closely related, separate them with a semicolon.
- If the second clause explains the first, separate them with a colon; if you want the second to be set off for emphasis, use a dash.
- Turn one of the independent clauses into a subordinate clause or modifier.

Practice 3

15. a. The subject is the implied you (refresh your memory in chapter 1). The subject performs the action of turning, so this is the active voice. In contrast, the subject in (b) is key. The key does not perform the action, but instead receives the action; that means it is in the passive voice.

16. b. The subject *Sheila* performs the action. In the first sentence, the subject *bank account* is acted upon by Sheila.

17. a. The action of the sentence is the verb *made,* and it is performed by the subject *we.* Sentence (b). uses *vacation plans* as its subject, and those plans do not *make* themselves.

Practice 4

18. yes. The emphasis is on the clock, not on the person who adjusted it.

19. no. Unless the context makes this necessary, this sentence is awkward, and should be rewritten in the active voice: *She unwrapped the gift.*

20. yes. The grandmother raised her grandchildren, but if we are focusing on Shauna and her brother, the passive is appropriate.

21. active

22. passive

23. active

The revised agent of action in each sentence is underlined.

24. A professional photographer took the pictures.

PRACTICE ANSWERS AND EXPLANATIONS *(cont'd)*

25. <u>Several children in the class</u> contracted the chicken pox.

26. a. The passive voice is more logical here because the agent of action (what delayed the train) is unknown.

27. a. The active voice is best here. The context doesn't provide reason to minimize the significance of *Alfonse* or to emphasize *your opinion*, and the agent of action is known.

Practice 5

28. *Displayed*, because the action is in the past.

29. After he drove for hours, my father stopped the car at a gas station. (The clause after the comma has been changed from the passive to the active voice.)

30. *Answered*, because the action takes place in the past.

31. *Will campaign*, because the action is going to take place in the future.

32. Because he didn't listen to the directions, he completed the assignment incorrectly. (The first phrase has been changed from passive to active.)

Practice 6

33. No. The modifier *useless* obviously refers to the present, not to the mother. The sentence should read, *Hernando gave a present that was useless to his mother*, or better yet, *Hernando gave a useless present to his mother.* (See the section on conciseness in chapter 4.)

34. No. *Considering the economy* is not something that a bank account can do. To make sense, the sentence should be *Considering the economy, I think my bank account is doing well.*

35. Yes. The modifiers *in front of* and *black* are correctly placed.

36. No. The modifier *that was hot* should be placed next to the noun it modifies, *coffee.*

37. No. While bookstores could place orders online, clearly the intended meaning is that the practice of ordering books online is hurting the sales of independent bookstores. A better sentence would be: *Independent bookstores are losing business because people order books online.* Or *Independent bookstores lose money when people order books online.*

PRACTICE ANSWERS AND EXPLANATIONS *(cont'd)*

Practice 7

38. This list could read "reading, skiing, and collecting." If stamp collecting isn't a hobby, that should be made clearer: "George's hobbies include reading and skiing. For a living, he collects international stamps."

39. You can't compare the flowers to Danson's shop. "The flowers from Becker's were fresher … than those from Danson's." Alternatively, "Becker's provides fresher flowers than Danson's."

40. The "neither…nor" structure requires parallel elements. "It was neither responsible nor respectful to leave the car blocking the way."

41. grammatical structure

42. comparable or analogous

43. giving them all the same grammatical structure

Answers may vary. The revised portion of the sentence is underlined.

44. At the party, the children stuffed themselves with cake and ice cream and <u>exhausted themselves with</u> backyard games.

45. Our foundation serves those who have been displaced because of natural disasters and <u>those who need shelter from abusive</u> <u>relationships</u>.

CHAPTER 2 QUIZ

For sentences 1–10, circle **T** for true or **F** for false.

1. **T F** Modifiers are said to dangle when there is nothing in the sentence for them to modify.

2. **T F** Pronoun shifts happen when a sentence begins with one subject and ends with two.

3. **T F** Use the passive voice when you want to emphasize the performer of the sentence's action.

4. **T F** In an inverted sentence, the verb follows the noun.

5. **T F** Most misplaced modifiers may be corrected by moving them closer to the word or phrase they are supposed to modify.

6. **T F** To correct a run-on sentence, place a comma between the two independent clauses.

7. **T F** Most nouns connected by *and* are treated as plural.

8. **T F** Verb tense shifts create a sense of action within a sentence.

9. **T F** Collective nouns take singular verbs even though they are made up of a number of individual units.

10. **T F** Sentence fragments are missing a verb or modifier.

For sentences 11–20, circle **C** for correct if there are no grammatical errors, and **I** for incorrect if there are. If you choose the latter, note the types of errors.

11. **C I** The Thomases, the Chius, and Joanne, bored with life in the country, is moving to the city.

    Error types:_____

12. **C I** That store's customer service was great; it helps me find just what I was looking for.

    Error types:_____

13. **C I** Learning to cook, my first dinner party was a
disaster.

Error types:_____

14. **C I** There's nothing like a cold glass of iced tea to refresh me
after a tennis game.

Error types:_____

15. **C I** After trying so many times to rid the computer of adware.

Error types:_____

16. **C I** Flying to the Caribbean, I thought about all the work I was
leaving behind.

Error types:_____

17. **C I** One of my favorite books is <u>The House of Mirth</u>, Edith
Wharton is an incredible writer.

Error types:_____

18. **C I** Why can't you take any of those overdue books back to the
library?

Error types:_____

19. **C I** Quinn bought a CD at the new music store that is at the
top of the charts.

Error types:_____

20. **C I** After Sarah failed to figure out what was wrong, the car
trouble was diagnosed by the mechanic.

Error types:_____

CHAPTER 2 QUIZ ANSWERS AND EXPLANATIONS

1. True.

2. False. Pronoun shifts are unnecessary changes between singular and plural; and among first, second, and third person.

3. False. Sentences written in the passive voice do not use the performer of the action as their subject.

4. False. In an inverted sentence, the noun follows the verb. For example, *There are many common grammatical errors.* The subject is *many common grammatical errors.*

5. True.

6. False. Such a comma is a grammatical error. Two independent clauses should be joined by an appropriate conjunction, separated by a semicolon, or divided into two sentences.

7. True.

8. False. Verb tense shifts are typically unnecessary and should be avoided unless deliberately changing reference to time periods.

9. True.

10. False. Sentence fragments are missing a subject or verb.

11. Incorrect; subject-verb agreement. The verb should be the plural *are*, because the subject is compound, consisting of *the Thomases, the Chius, and Joanne.*

12. Incorrect; unnecessary shift. The verb *helps* should be in the past tense because the first part of the sentence is in the past (*was great*) and there is no reason to change the tense.

13. Incorrect; dangling modifier. The phrase *learning to cook* has nothing to modify (the dinner party was not learning to cook).

CHAPTER 2 ANSWERS AND EXPLANATIONS *(cont'd)*

14. Correct.

15. Incorrect; sentence fragment. There is no subject or verb. This phrase would function better as a modifier. For example, *He gave up after trying so many times to rid the computer of adware.*

16. Correct.

17. Incorrect; run-on sentence. Two independent clauses should not be joined by a comma; they should be joined by a semicolon or made into two sentences.

18. Correct.

19. Incorrect; misplaced modifier. The store isn't at the top of the charts; the CD is. That modifying phrase should be moved closer the word it modifies: *At the new music store, Quinn bought a CD that is at the top of the charts.*

20. Incorrect; unnecessary passive voice. The emphasis of the sentence is on who diagnosed the car trouble. The passive voice instead places emphasis on the problem. The active voice should be used: *After Sarah failed to figure out what was wrong, the mechanic diagnosed the car trouble*

CHAPTER 3

Punctuation

BUILDING BLOCK QUIZ

For questions 1–5, determine which underlined portion(s) of each sentence contains an error (a blank line may indicate missing punctuation).

1. Time was up, however, Gail still had 20 questions left_ to answer.
          (A)   (B)   (C)

2. Such a small <u>amount</u> of caffeine_ shouldn't have any <u>affect</u> on
                (A)   (B)   (C)
   <u>your</u> ability to fall asleep tonight.
   (D)

3. Chuck <u>felt</u> really <u>bad</u> when Xu Mei started <u>to cry</u>, and he
       (A)   (B)   (C)
   decided never to tease her_ again.
                     (D)

4. *Jade*_ Horace's favorite novel_ is being made into a movie_
   (A)   (B)   (C)
   starring his favorite actor.

5. By the time the dinner party was over_ it was well past
                                (A)
   midnight, and_ everyone was exhausted
   (B)   (C)

For questions 6–8, choose the best version of each sentence. If the original is best, choose (A).

6. Safe popular freedom consists of four things, the diffusion of liberty, of intelligence, of property, and of conscientiousness. —*Joseph Cook*

   (A) No change

   (B) Safe popular freedom consists of four things, the diffusion of: liberty, intelligence, property, and conscientiousness.

   (C) Safe popular freedom consists of four things: the diffusion of liberty, of intelligence, of property, and of conscientiousness.

   (D) Safe popular freedom consists of four things: the diffusion of liberty; of intelligence; of property; and of conscientiousness.

7. Frank Scully said, "Why not go out on a limb? Isn't that where the fruit is"?

   (A) No change

   (B) Frank Scully said: "Why not go out on a limb? Isn't that where the fruit is"?

   (C) Frank Scully said; "Why not go out on a limb? Isn't that where the fruit is?"

   (D) Frank Scully said, "Why not go out on a limb? Isn't that where the fruit is?"

8. Either I will find a way: or I will make one. —*Sir Philip Sidney*

   (A) No change

   (B) Either I will find a way—or I will make one.

   (C) Either I will find a way, or I will make one.

   (D) Either I will find a way; or I will make one.

For questions 9–10, identify which underlined portion (if any) contains an error. If there is no error, choose (E)

9. Well, if I have to choose right now, I guess I'll pick...that one
      (A)   (B)   (C)

   over there. No error
      (D)   (E)

10. The pitcher <u>threw</u> a curve ball<u>.</u> Quintero swung with all his
  (A) (B)

might<u>!</u> It was a grand slam<u>!</u> <u>No error</u>
  (C) (D) (E)

BUILDING BLOCK QUIZ ANSWERS AND EXPLANATIONS

1. A This is a run-on; a comma is not strong enough to separate independent clauses without a coordinating conjunction (*however* is a conjunctive adverb; see chapter 1).

2. C *Affect* is a verb; *effect* is a noun and is the correct word for this sentence.

3. B *Bad* is an adjective; this sentence needs the adverb *badly* to modify *felt*.

4. A and B That the novel is Horace's favorite is not essential to the sentence, so set it off with commas.

5. A The clause *by the time the dinner party was over* introduces the main action of the sentence, so set it off with a comma.

6. C Because the list follows a complete thought, it should be introduced by a colon, not a comma, (A) and (B). There is no comma in any of the items in the list, so the items should not be separated by semicolons (D).

7. D Quotations introduced by *said* should usually be preceded by a comma, not a colon, (A) and (B), or semicolon (C). (A) and (B) also incorrectly put the question mark outside the quotation marks.

8. B A colon introduces lists, quotations, and explanations; it should not separate independent clauses (A). (B) and (C) are both correct; either a comma or a dash effectively separate independent clauses with a coordinating conjunction. Given the nature of the quotation, however, (B) is more emphatic and therefore more effective. A semicolon is incorrect when two clauses are connected by a coordinating conjunction.

9. E There is no error. The ellipsis (…) is correctly used to show hesitation in speech.

10. C   The exclamation point is overused. It is effective after the last sentence.

THE VALUE OF PUNCTUATION

Writing that is otherwise powerful and clear can be mangled by misplaced commas, misspelled words, and incorrect capitals—the subjects of this final section.

Many writers consider punctuation an instrument of torture, but it really *is* designed to help express ideas clearly:

> **a**. I know who did it, Winston.
>
> **b**. I know who did it: Winston.

Punctuation clarifies ideas and signals relationships between them. In **a**, the speaker tells Winston that she knows who did it; in **b**, the speaker says *Winston* did it. Effective punctuation can also add vigor, conveying emotion and tone:

> Don't do that!
>
> That tie is a little … colorful, don't you think?

We'll cover all of punctuation in this chapter; the next chapter will be devoted to capitalization and spelling.

WHEN TO USE A COMMA

The comma is the most common punctuation mark; it gently separates sentence elements from each other or from the main clause. Here are its seven rules.

1. Between two independent clauses connected by a coordinating conjunction

Place the comma at the end of the first clause *before* the coordinating conjunction. If both clauses are short and there's no chance for confusion, you can omit the comma. On the other hand, you may want to keep that comma for effect.

> Anuj always loved animals, so I'm not surprised that he is a veterinarian.
> I love you and you love me.
> I love you, but you don't love me.

FLASHBACK

A comma alone isn't strong enough to stand between two independent clauses; it must be paired with a coordinating conjunction (*and, or, nor, for, so, but* and *yet*).

---

2. After an introductory word, phrase, or clause

Introductory words, phrases, and clauses are typically adverbs that tell us the when, where, why, how or under what conditions the action of the sentence took place. They should always be followed by a comma.

> Unfortunately, the roster is already full.
> Without a cup of coffee, I'm useless in the morning.

In the last example, a subordinate clause introduces the main clause. But be careful: a subordinate clause at the beginning of a sentence does not always serve that function:

> **Incorrect**:   Whoever ate my lunch, is going to pay!

This subordinate clause is the subject of the main clause, so the comma is wrong.

Practice 1

Insert any necessary commas in the following sentences.

1. I wanted to call you right away but I didn't want to wake you so I decided to wait until the morning.

2. Whatever you decide I will support you for you are my best friend.

3. Between items in a series

Three or more items in a series should be separated by commas. This includes a comma between the last two items (but *not* a comma after the last item). Some consider this penultimate comma optional, but it's best to play it safe and use the comma to clearly separate the two items.

> The <u>sandhill crane,</u> <u>American alligator,</u> and West Indian manatee are all endangered Florida wetland species.

When one or more items in the series itself has a comma, use semicolons to separate the items in the list.

4. Between adjectives that modify the same word

Coordinate adjectives modify the same noun or pronoun; they must be separated by commas:

> The <u>dark, dingy room</u> could use a coat of bright paint.

MEMORY TIP

If you can logically insert the word *and* between two consecutive adjectives, there should be a comma between them.

Cumulative adjectives build up to one modifying phrase and do not take commas:

> The <u>light blue paint</u> really brightens the room.

Cumulative: The <u>fierce north wind</u> threatened to knock over the old barn.

Coordinate: The <u>fierce, steady wind</u> threatened to knock over the old barn.

Practice 2

Insert any necessary commas in the following sentences.

3. Neither rain nor sleet nor hail nor a plague of grasshoppers will keep me from Miller's one-day sale.

4. The only thing we had to eat was watery vegetable soup.

5. To set off nonessential modifiers

Appositives and adjective phrases or clauses should be set off with commas if they are not essential to the meaning of the sentence.

An **appositive** is a modifier that defines or renames another noun (much like a subject complement defines or renames the subject).

Adjective phrase: Henry Ford, openly challenging his own role as a history maker, once said, "History is bunk."

Adjective clause: Henry Ford, who is one of the most important figures in American history, once said, "History is bunk."

Appositive: Henry Ford, one of the most important figures in American history, once said, "History is bunk."

Essential elements are not set off by commas. Without the information in the phrase, clause, or appositive, the sentence loses its specific meaning.

The documents <u>signed by Henry Ford</u> fetched $2,000 each at the auction.

> **REMEMBER THIS!**
>
> Any information that is essential (that limits the meaning of the sentence) should **not** be set off by commas.

Practice 3

Insert any necessary commas in the following sentences.

5. My cousin Mikala who has been suffering from back pain for years swears that acupuncture has cured her.

6. The package that I needed for the meeting had been delivered to the wrong address.

6. To set off transitional and parenthetical expressions, question tags, affirmatives and negatives, and mild interjections

Transitions

Transitional words and phrases link sentences or parts of sentences, showing the relationship between them (e.g., comparison or cause and effect).

Wolhee's grandfather, for example, was a master potter in Korea.

Parenthetical expressions

A parenthetical expression offers ancillary information or acts as an afterthought that interrupts or concludes the sentence.

The wipers need to be replaced, you know.

Question tags

Question tags are exactly that: questions we tack on to the end of a sentence.

You're coming with us, aren't you?

Affirmatives and negatives

Words or phrases indicating acceptance or rejection should also be set off from the main sentence.

On second thought, no, Haily and Jules would not make good lab partners.

Mild interjections and other interrupters

Strong interjections stand alone as short sentences ending in an exclamation point (e.g., *Back off!*); but mild interjections are usually part of a sentence and are separated by a comma. Mild or casual interrupters such as *um, like,* and *well* follow the same rule.

Hey, isn't that Old Man Morrison's dog running down the street?

7. To set off quotations, dates, and addresses

Direct address

In a direct address, the specific person being addressed should be set off by commas.

> We should grill Huang since it's such a nice day outside.
>
> We should grill, Huang, since it's such a nice day outside.

This is essential for clarity; without the commas, we might grill Huang.

Direct quotation

When you quote someone else's words, set them off with commas as well as quotation marks. *Indirect* quotes should have neither commas nor quotation marks:

> **Direct**:   Omar said, "Ted, I really need your help."
>
> **Indirect**:   Omar told Ted he really needs his help.

Quotations consisting of more than four lines are usually introduced by colons instead of commas.

> **REMEMBER THIS!**
>
> Direct address and direct quotations get commas; indirect quotations do not.

Dates

Place commas around the year, unless the date is inverted or only the month and year are stated:

> On February 11, 1998, Lukas was born.
>
> April 2000 was the rainiest month in this town's history.

Addresses

Use commas to separate the street from the town, the town from the state or province, and the state or province from the country.

> His mailing address is 2234 Vine Street, Oak Ridge, PA 19042.

Practice 4

Insert any necessary commas in the following sentences.

7. We have lots of time to kill Eddie so what should we do?

8. "Please excuse me" Joel said and then he raced out of the room.

9. I met my husband at Waterloo Lounge in Watertown New York in January 2001.

10. Noam Feighter AIA was the chief architect for the building at 3305 Main Street in Red Rock Arkansas.

SEMICOLON

The semicolon's form actually reflects its function. Like a period, the semicolon separates two independent clauses; like a comma, it keeps them connected.

Between Two Independent Clauses

Two closely related independent clauses can be joined by a semicolon:

> The polls suggest we are losing ground with young voters; however, our level of support from all other demographic groups remains strong.

> **FLASHBACK**
>
> Common conjunctive adverbs include *however, therefore, furthermore, similarly, still,* and *thus* (see chapter 1).

If one clause is independent and the other subordinate, a semicolon will create a sentence fragment. If the clauses are not closely related, they should not be connected:

Incorrect: The first Oscars were awarded in 1927; this year, the nominees for best picture include three historical films.

In this case, even a coordinating conjunction isn't wise; the best punctuation between these two sentences is a period.

Practice 5

Determine whether the semicolon is correct and appropriate in each of the following sentences.

11. You don't get ulcers from what you eat; you get ulcers from what's eating you. —*Anonymous*

12. A failure is not always a mistake; it may simply be the best one can do under the circumstances. —*B.F. Skinner*

REMEMBER THIS!

Note that the key to correct use of the semicolon is twofold: (1) *both* clauses must be independent and (2) the sentences must be closely related.

When Not to Use a Semicolon

Semicolons are easy to misuse. **Do not** use a semicolon:

1. Between independent clauses joined by a coordinating conjunction. Use a comma or change the coordinating conjunction to a conjunctive adverb.

   Incorrect: I usually drink coffee; but today I'm drinking tea.

2. Between a subordinate and independent clause. Semicolons join grammatically equivalent parts. A subordinate clause and independent clause are not grammatically equal. Use a comma or make both clauses independent.

   Incorrect: Although I usually drink coffee; today I'm drinking tea.

3. To introduce a list. If there's any punctuation at all, it should be a colon (see the next section).

   Incorrect: Bela's list of favorite bands includes; Coldplay; Ween; and Crosby, Stills, Nash, and Young.

Practice 6

Determine whether each space should be filled by a comma or a semicolon, or left blank.

13. Never be haughty to the humble_ never be humble to the haughty.
    —*Jefferson Davis*

14. It's great to be great_ but it's greater to be human. —*Will Rogers*

COLON

The colon's main function is to introduce quotations, lists, summaries, or explanations.

Introducing Quotations

Quotations introduced by an independent clause should be preceded by a colon.

> According to Maria Tatar, the power of fairy tales lies in their ability to help us cope: "Fairy tales register an effort to develop maps for coping with personal anxieties."

If the quotation is introduced by a phrase or subordinate clause, use a comma if necessary; otherwise, no punctuation is needed.

> According to Maria Tatar, "[f]airy tales register an effort to develop maps for coping with personal anxieties."

> Maria Tatar states that "[f]airy tales register an effort to develop maps for coping with personal anxieties."

If the quotation is introduced with *said* or other words of dialogue, use a comma, not a colon, even if the introduction is a full sentence.

> **Incorrect:** Professor Grimes said: "Pay particular attention to word choice in this poem."

Introducing Lists

If a list is introduced by an independent clause, separate the clause and list with a colon:

> Be sure to pack the following items: a sleeping bag, a flashlight, bug spray, and a canteen.

However, do not use a colon to introduce

1. a series of objects or complements following a verb,

2. a series of objects following a preposition, or

3. a list introduced by *such as*, *including*, or *for example* (these words already introduce, so a colon is redundant).

Practice 7

Determine whether the colons in the following sentences are correct.

15. Henry L. Doherty said: "It is the studying that you do after your school days that really counts."

16. According to Henry L. Doherty: "It is the studying that you do after your school days that really counts."

Introducing Summaries or Explanations

Use a colon to introduce a word, phrase, or clause that summarizes or explains the preceding sentence. When what follows a colon is a complete clause, the first letter should be capitalized.

> The Allies' mission was twofold: to halt the advance of German troops near the capital and to open up a safe supply route to the city.

> If you smoke, I have but one word of advice: Quit.

Don't insert a colon before a summary or explanation that is a subject complement.

> **Incorrect**: Luck is: an accident that happens to the competent.
> —*Albert M. Greenfield*

Practice 8

Correct any colon, semicolon, or comma errors in the following sentences.

17. The tongue is: more to be feared than the sword.
    —*Japanese proverb*

18. Experience is the worst teacher, it gives the test before presenting the lesson. —*Vernon Law*

DASH

A favorite punctuation mark of many writers, the dash is often used in places where a comma, semicolon, colon, or parenthesis would also be correct.

> We were alone—all alone at last—and I was too nervous to tell her how I feel.

> We were alone, all alone at last, and I was too nervous to tell her how I feel.

The dashes emphasize the writer's emotions; the commas are correct, but deflating. Don't overuse the dash: that defeats its purpose and makes your writing choppy.

To Set off Appositives with Commas

Appositives—nouns or noun phrases that rename nearby nouns—should generally be set off by commas. But if an appositive contains commas, use dashes.

> Everything that I'd packed—my suitcases, my golf clubs, and a box of presents—was lost by the airline.

Practice 9

Correct any inappropriate uses of the dash in the following sentences.

19. You do not lead by hitting people over the head—that's assault, not leadership. —*Dwight D. Eisenhower*

20. Conscience is the inner voice that warns us—that someone may be looking. —*H.L. Mencken*

QUOTATION MARKS

Quotation marks have three main functions:

To Set Off Direct Quotations

Any **direct** quotation—of a person, book, article, song, etc.—should be enclosed in quotation marks.

> Eric Hoffer said, "We lie loudest when we lie to ourselves."

Direct vs. Indirect Quotations

Be sure to distinguish between direct and indirect quotations. Indirect quotations *are not* enclosed in quotation marks.

> **Direct:** Ivy said, "Did you know a ten-minute shower uses 50 gallons of water?"
>
> **Indirect:** According to Ivy, a ten-minute shower uses 50 gallons of water.

Long Quotations

When quoting poetry or prose and the quotation is more than four full lines of text or more than three lines of poetry, omit the quotation marks. Instead, indent the quotation.

> In Anne Sexton's version of "Little Red Riding Hood," deception itself, not the wolf, is the true villain:
>
> > The wolf, they decided, was too mean
> > to be simply shot so they filled his belly
> > with large stones and sewed him up.
> > He was as heavy as a cemetery
> > and when he woke up and tried to run off
> > he fell over dead. Killed by his own weight.
> > Many a deception ends on such a note.

Quotations within Quotations

A quotation that appears within a quotation is set off using single quotes.

> In his August 2003 article in *The Nation*, Joe Conason explains the term "compassionate conservative": "'Compassionate' softens 'conservative,' a word that tends to be associated with smug stinginess."

Practice 10

Correct any quotation mark errors in the following sentences.

21. According to Juanita Lawes, "Frankenstein's greatest error was not in creating the creature but in abandoning him, leaving him a "miserable wretch" forever."

22. Piu said "his favorite novel is *Frankenstein*."

Around Titles

Titles of short works or portions of long works should appear in quotation marks. Short works include: newspaper and magazine articles, short stories, poems, chapters or sections of books, songs, episodes of television or radio programs.

Thus, the title of Bob Dylan's song "Tangled Up in Blue" should be in quotation marks while the album title, *Blood on the Tracks*, belongs in italics.

Quotation Marks and Other Punctuation Marks

One common area of confusion is where to place other punctuation marks when you have a quotation. Fortunately, there are only two rules:

1. In American usage, periods and commas always go **inside** the quotation marks.

   "I need a new job," Juno said. "This one is driving me crazy."

2. Colons, semicolons, dashes, question marks and exclamation marks go **inside** if they are part of the quotation and **outside** if they apply to the whole sentence.

   Colin said excitedly, "There it is!"—and there it was, barely visible: the Statue of Liberty.

   Harrison wrote, "Dear Jane: I cannot tell you how deeply you hurt me"; then he tore up the paper and threw it away, deciding it was best to speak to Jane in person.

Practice 11

Insert quotation marks where needed in the following sentences.

23. Read Chapter 3: Invertebrates for next class.

24. The Love Song of J. Alfred Prufrock is one of T. S. Eliot's most famous poems.

END MARKS

The Period

All sentences except direct questions and exclamations should end in a period.

> **Statement**: It's getting late.
>
> **Statement**: Géza wants to know if you're ready to go. (indirect question)

The Question Mark

A direct question should be followed by a question mark. If you have a series of questions, each question can be followed by a question mark, even if each question is not a complete sentence.

> **Indirect**: Cameron asked who is in charge around here.
>
> **Direct**: "Who is in charge around here?" Cameron asked.
>
> **Series**: Did you pack your pajamas? Your toothbrush? Your medication?

REMEMBER THIS!

Only use question marks for direct questions.

The Exclamation Point

Genuine exclamations—words, phrases, or clauses that express strong emotions or forceful commands—take the exclamation point as their end mark.

This is the most exciting day of my life!

"Duck!" Melinda yelled as Chet threw an icy snowball toward my head.

In the second example, the quotation gets the exclamation point, not the entire sentence—and the exclamation point is inside the quotation marks.

Don't overuse the exclamation point. It is generally considered informal (commonly used in comic strips, for example), and overuse will reduce the impact of true exclamations.

Practice 12

Correct any errors in end mark punctuation in the sentences below.

25. You don't know where you're going, do you.

26. Juanita asked me whether I thought it was a good idea?

> **FLASHBACK**
>
> Remember, end marks go inside quotation marks.

Periods in Abbreviations

The period is also used in many abbreviations.

Period(s)	
Social titles: **Mr., Mrs., Ms., Jr., Sr.**	Time references: **B.C., B.C.E., A.D.; a.m.**
Professional titles or rank: **Dr., R.N., D.D.S., Sgt.**	Latin abbreviations: **i.e., e.g., vs., et al., etc.**
Academic titles: **B.A., M.A., Ph.D.**	Quantities or measurements: **lb., in., oz., no.**

No Period(s)	
State names: **PA, CA, TX**	Organization names: **UN, FTC, NASA, NAACP, CIA**

There are no spaces after the periods in abbreviations. When in doubt about an abbreviation, consult a dictionary or style guide. Here are some notes on using abbreviations correctly:

1. If a sentence ends in an abbreviation that uses a period, do not add another period.

   Incorrect: Someday, I will be Bakhtan Balarasan, <u>Ph.D..</u>

2. Do not abbreviate titles *unless* they appear with a name.

   Incorrect: My <u>dr.</u> said I should stay in bed for about a week.

   Correct: <u>My doctor</u> said I should stay in bed for about a week.

3. To use an abbreviation that isn't familiar to your readers, write out the full word(s) followed by the abbreviation in parentheses; thereafter you may use the abbreviation.

   Incorrect: The <u>AFWA</u> reports an unusual weather pattern over the North Pole.

   Correct: The <u>Air Force Weather Agency (AFWA)</u> reports an unusual weather pattern over the North Pole.

4. Use time and number abbreviations only with specific numbers.

   Incorrect: Kobe wakes early every <u>a.m.</u>

   Correct: Kobe wakes at <u>6 a.m.</u> every morning.

5. Avoid informal abbreviations of days of the week, months, measurements, names, states, company names, and academic subjects.

   Incorrect: Ty <u>Bros. Co.</u> has a big <u>Xmas</u> sale each <u>Dec.</u>

   Correct: Ty <u>Brothers Company</u> has a big <u>Christmas</u> sale each <u>December</u>.

Practice 13

Correct any errors in abbreviations in the following sentences.

27. Tamar earned her BS degree in just three yrs.

28. Maj Wrubleski has a reputation for being especially tough on new recruits.

THE APOSTROPHE

The apostrophe has two uses you know well: to show possession and omission.

Possessives

Most nouns and indefinite pronouns (e.g., *someone, anybody*) show possession by adding the apostrophe and –*s*.

Uncle Ming's homemade dumplings were the hit of the party.

Nouns ending in –s

For singular nouns ending in –*s*, add both the apostrophe and –*s* unless the pronunciation will be awkward.

The witness's statement sounded forced.

For plural nouns ending in –*s*, only add the apostrophe.

The witnesses' statements corroborated the defendant's story.

Joint possession and compound nouns

When two or more nouns share possession of an item, add the apostrophe only to the last noun. However, if each individual possesses the item, show possession for each noun.

Individual: Roxanne's and *Ravi's* dogs won prizes in the dog show. [Roxanne and Ravi each own dogs.]

Joint: Roxanne and Ravi's dogs won prizes in the dog show. [Roxanne and Ravi jointly own the dogs.]

To Show Omission

Use the apostrophe when you omit one or more letters from a word or numbers from a date.

I can't believe you're going without me.

Say what you like about disco; I still love the music of the '70s.

Incorrect Uses

Avoid the following common misuses of the apostrophe.

1. **To form plurals.** Plurals are formed *only* with *–s* (or *–es*)—not with an apostrophe.

   Incorrect: The <u>dog's</u> chased the cat up the tree.

2. **With possessive pronouns.** The possessive pronouns (*mine, yours, his, whose,* etc.) already show possession; to add an apostrophe is both incorrect and redundant (see chapters 1 and 14).

   Incorrect: Is this jacket <u>your's</u> or <u>her's</u>?

3. **With plural numbers and letters**. Don't use the apostrophe to make plural numbers and letters. Use only the plural *-s* or *–es* for numbers. To make a letter plural, italicize or capitalize the letter and add *–s* or *–es* unless the result is a word. In that case, use the apostrophe to prevent confusion.

   Incorrect: There are two <u>10's</u> missing from this deck of cards.

   Correct: There are two <u>10s</u> missing from this deck of cards.

   Incorrect: Both of the <u>M's</u> had faded, so the sign read "Toy's" instead of "Tommy's."

   Correct: Both of the <u>Ms</u> had faded, so the sign read "Toy's" instead of "Tommy's."

   Correct: There are four <u>i's</u> and four <u>s's</u> in *Mississippi*. [Without the apostrophe, readers might mistake *is* for *is;* use the apostrophe for both letters for consistency.]

Practice 14

Correct any apostrophe errors in the following sentences.

29. Alanas résumé is very impressive, isnt it?

30. The 1980's is known as the "me" decade.

ALL THE REST

Parentheses

Parentheses set off information that is supplemental or tangential—a minor example, a digression, an afterthought. Parentheses are also used for numbering items in a list as well as for citation material.

> My brother has many nicknames (including Bullfrog, Tadpole, and T-Man, to name a few), but he only ever answers to the name Eugene.
>
> Which would you rather have: (a) $1,000,000 in one lump sum or (b) $100,000 a year for life?
>
> The fiscal crisis that ensued was due "solely to the greed of a few top managers" (Jacobs 113).

Formal writing should contain few parenthetical thoughts. As you revise, see how many of your parenthetical ideas can be worked into the text or omitted.

Brackets ([ ])

Brackets indicate that you have added words to, or changed words in, a quotation. Brackets also indicate stage directions in a play. As you've seen over and over in this text, brackets can also set off special instructions or explanations.

Practice 15

Correct any errors in the use of parentheses or brackets in the following sentences.

31. Do you want to 1. go to the movies, 2. go out to dinner, or 3. both?

32. In the final scene, Joy [crying softly] confesses to Hitch (her dying son), "Dylan (Hitch's coach) is your real father, and he's loved you more than you'll ever know."

Ellipsis (…)

Ellipsis has two uses: (1) to indicate that you have deleted one or more words from a quotation and (2) to indicate hesitation, interruption, or unfinished thought in speech. (If you delete a full sentence or more from a quotation, use an additional period after the ellipsis.)

SUMMARY

DO use a **comma:**

1. between two independent clauses connected by a coordinating conjunction
2. after an introductory word, phrase, or clause
3. between items in a series
4. between adjectives that modify the same word
5. to set off nonessential modifiers
6. to set off transitional and parenthetical expressions, question tags, affirmatives and negatives, and mild interjections
7. to set off a direct address or direct quotation
8. to separate parts of dates, numbers, addresses, and titles
9. as needed to prevent confusion.

Semicolons are used primarily to separate independent clauses that are closely related. They can be connected with or without a transitional word or phrase.

Colons have three major functions: to introduce quotations, lists, and summaries or explanations that are introduced by an independent clause. If the quotation is introduced by *said*, use a comma. Never use a colon between a verb and its objects or complement, between a preposition and its object, or after *such as*, *including*, and *for example*.

Minor functions of the colon include separating a salutation from the body of the letter, separating hours and minutes, showing ratios or proportions, separating titles and subtitles, and separating city and publisher in a bibliography.

The **dash** sets off words, phrases or clauses for emphasis. It should be used sparingly, only when an idea really deserves to be set off.

Finally, **quotation marks** set off direct quotations, titles of short works, and words being used in a special way within sentences. Long quotations should be indented and quotation marks omitted. If you have a quotation within a quotation, use single quotation marks (') for the internal quotation. Periods and commas always go inside quotation marks; semicolons, colons, dashes, question marks, and exclamation points go inside the quotation marks only if they are part of the quotation.

Most sentences should end in a **period**. A sentence that asks a direct question should end in a **question mark**. Sentences that express strong emotion (e.g., interjections) or forceful commands should end in an **exclamation point**.

Periods are used in many **abbreviations**. In general, abbreviations of social, professional, and academic titles; time references; Latin abbreviations; and quantities or measurements should have periods. Sentences ending in an abbreviation with a period do not take another period. Titles should only be abbreviated if used with names. Unfamiliar abbreviations should be written out first, with the abbreviation in parentheses. Time and number abbreviations should only be used with specific numbers, and informal abbreviations (e.g., *Mon.* or *phys. ed.*) should be avoided.

Apostrophes show possession and omission. To show possession, add an apostrophe and –*s* (if the noun is plural and ends in –*s*, or if adding –*s* to a singular noun ending in –*s* makes an awkward pronunciation, add only the apostrophe). To show joint possession, add the apostrophe only to the last noun. Do not use the apostrophe to make plurals or with possessive pronouns, except to prevent confusion.

Parentheses set off supplemental or tangential information. **Brackets** indicate added words or changed words in a quotation, and set off stage directions in a play.

Ellipsis indicates omitted words in a quotation, or hesitation or interruption in speech.

Practice: On Your Own

Choose a magazine or book and look for examples of each comma rule. You can also search for examples of superfluous commas. Check samples of your own writing, letters you receive, or websites such as blogs.

PRACTICE ANSWERS AND EXPLANATIONS

Practice 1

1. I wanted to call you right away, but I didn't want to wake you, so I decided to wait until the morning. [Comma between independent clauses; it would be acceptable to omit the first comma as both clauses are short.]

2. Whatever you decide, I will support you, for you are my best friend. [Comma after the introductory clause and between the two independent clauses]

Practice 2

3. Neither rain, nor sleet, nor hail, nor a plague of grasshoppers will keep me from Miller's one-day sale. [Comma between items in the series]

4. The only thing we had to eat was watery vegetable soup. [No comma between cumulative adjectives; vegetable describes soup]

Practice 3

5. My cousin Mikala, who has been suffering from back pain for years, swears that acupuncture has cured her. [Commas around nonessential clause]

6. The package that I needed for the meeting had been delivered to the wrong address. [No comma; the clause is essential]

Practice 4

7. We have lots of time to kill, Eddie, so what should we do? [Commas around direct address and between independent clauses]

8. "Please excuse me," Joel said, and then he raced out of the room. [Comma after direct quotation and between independent clauses]

9. I met my husband at Waterloo Lounge in Watertown, New York, in January 2001. [Commas around the state; no comma between month and year when no day is included]

PRACTICE ANSWERS AND EXPLANATIONS *(cont'd)*

10. Noam Feighter, AIA, was the chief architect for the building at 3305 Main Street in Red Rock, Arkansas. [Commas around title and between town and state]

Practice 5

11. Yes. Both clauses are independent and directly related.

12. Yes. Both clauses are independent and directly related.

Practice 6

13. Semicolon. Both clauses are independent and there is no coordinating conjunction, so a comma would create a sentence fragment.

14. Comma. The independent clauses are connected by a coordinating conjunction, so a comma is the correct punctuation mark.

Practice 7

15. No. Use a comma with the *he said* construction.

16. No. The introduction is only a phrase, so the punctuation mark should be a comma.

Practice 8

17. Delete the colon; do not use a colon to introduce an explanation that is a subject complement.

18. The comma creates a sentence fragment because it stands alone between two independent clauses. A semicolon would be correct since the clauses are closely related. A colon is even more correct as the second clause explains the first (telling us *why* experience is the worst teacher).

Practice 9

19. The dash is appropriate.

20. The dash is unnecessary. Why separate the subordinate clause? It is especially awkward because the clause is essential to the sentence.

PRACTICE ANSWERS AND EXPLANATIONS *(cont'd)*

Practice 10

21. The quotation marks around *miserable wretch* and *become linked to the chain of existence* should be single quotation marks (') since they are quotations within a quotation.

22. This is an indirect quotation, so there shouldn't be any quotation marks.

Practice 11

23. Read "Chapter 3: Invertebrates" for next class.

24. "The Love Song of J. Alfred Prufrock" is one of T. S. Eliot's most famous poems.

Practice 12

25. You don't know where you're going, do you? [This is a direct question and should end in a question mark. (Note the comma setting off the question tag.)]

26. Juanita asked me whether I thought it was a good idea. [This is a statement, not a question, so it should end in a period.]

Practice 13

27. Tamar earned her <u>B.S.</u> degree in just three <u>years</u>. [Use periods in academia degrees and avoid informal abbreviations.]

28. <u>Maj.</u> Wrubleski has a reputation for being especially tough on new recruits. [Use periods for title abbreviations.]

Practice 14

29. <u>Alana's</u> résumé is very impressive, <u>isn't</u> it? [*Alana's* is possessive, not plural; *isn't* is a contraction needing an apostrophe.]

30. The <u>1980s</u> is known as the "me" decade. [No apostrophes for decades or other numbers.]

PRACTICE ANSWERS AND EXPLANATIONS *(cont'd)*

Practice 15

31. Do you want to (1) go to the movies, (2) go out to dinner, or (3) both? [Put parentheses around the numbers; the periods create confusion.]

32. In the final scene, Joy, crying softly, confesses to Hitch, her dying son, "Dylan [Hitch's teacher] is your real father, and he's loved you more than you'll ever know." [The brackets are incorrect; though the sentence discusses a play, these are not stage directions. The first parentheses can be replaced by commas for an appositive. The parentheses in the quotation should be brackets.]

CHAPTER 3 QUIZ

For questions 1–3, determine where in the sentence a comma(s) needs to be placed.

1. A kiss can be_ a comma_ a question mark_ or an exclamation
          (A)   (B)   (C)

    point. —*Mistinguett*

2. That_ must be fine_ for_ I don't understand a word. —*Molière*
        (A)   (B) (C)

3. All meanings_ we know_ depend_ on the key of interpretation.
              (A)   (B)   (C)

    —*George Eliot*

For questions 4–5, determine which commas, if any, are superfluous.

4. Is it possible for contestants on a reality show‚ to be themselves‚
                                                 (A)   (B)

    or are they always acting?"‚ Joachim asked.
                           (C)

5. With tears in his eyes, the defendant told the jurors, he was
              (A)   (B)
    deeply sorry, for what he'd done.
              (C)

For questions 6–13, is the punctuation correct in each of the following? How might you improve it?

6. Life is the greatest bargain, we get it for nothing. —*Yiddish proverb*

7. Doing what you like is freedom, liking what you do is happiness. —*Frank Tyger*

8. Some people grow under responsibility: others merely swell. —*Carl Hubbell*

9. Never mind your happiness, do your duty.—*Will Durant*

10. What did Lindsay mean when she said "We need to take a break?"

11. The editorial Justice for Mall is worth reading.

12. Never to have changed—what a pitiable thing of which to boast! —*Johann Wolfgang von Goethe*

13. If you look closely, you will see, that the numbers increase at a ratio of 1–3.

For questions 14–20, dentify which change, if any, is needed to correct each sentence.

14. Our cat UFO (short for Unique Feline Organism) licked it's paws and curled up on the pillow, purring contentedly.

    (A) Put *UFO* in the parentheses.

    (B) Change *it's* to *its*.

    (C) Change *paws* to *paw's*.

    (D) Insert periods in *UFO*.

    (E) No change

15. Dear Mr. Holmes: Enclosed please find a copy of my invoice from Sept. Please remit ASAP as the invoice is now several months past due. Thx.

    (A) Write out *Sept.*, *ASAP*, and *Thx.*
    (B) Write out only *ASAP.*
    (C) Insert periods between letters in *ASAP.*
    (D) Change *Thx* to *thank you.*
    (E) No change

16. Carlito tried to open the door, but it was locked! So was the other one! How was he going to get out?

    (A) Change the question mark to an exclamation mark.
    (B) Change the first exclamation point to a period.
    (C) Change both exclamation points to periods.
    (D) Change both exclamation points to question marks.
    (E) No change

17. I want a car that gets at least 18 m.p.g. and that I can finance at a reasonable APR.

    (A) Change *APR* to *A.P.R.*
    (B) Change *m.p.g.* to *mpg.*
    (C) Change *APR* to *A.P.R.* and add a period at the end of the sentence.
    (D) Change *m.p.g.* to *miles per gallon* and *APR* to *rate.*
    (E) No change

18. After surveying both crime scenes, Det. Mombasa had no doubt that the two robberies were the work of the same thief.

    (A) Change *Det.* to *det.*
    (B) Change *Det.* to *detective.*
    (C) Change *scenes* to *scene's.*
    (D) Change *were* to *we're.*
    (E) No change

19. "We're goin fishin," Bubba said "Do you wanna come?"

    (A) Move the comma outside the quotation mark.

    (B) Add apostrophes to the end of *goin* and *fishin*.

    (C) Delete the apostrophe in *we're*.

    (D) Move the question mark outside the quotation mark.

    (E) No change

20. "Giles needs to take his p.m. medicine," Patricia told the R.N. on duty.

    (A) Change *p.m.* to *evening* and *R.N.* to *nurse*.

    (B) Change *p.m.* to *pm* and *R.N.* to *RN*.

    (C) Change *p.m.* to *P.M.*

    (D) Move the comma outside of the quotation mark.

    (E) No change

CHAPTER 3 QUIZ ANSWERS AND EXPLANATIONS

1. B and C   Items in a series should be set off by commas.

2. B   Insert a comma between independent clauses connected by a coordinating conjunction.

3. A and B   The parenthetical expression *we know* interrupts the sentence and should be set off by commas.

4. A and C   (A) has a superfluous comma between a subject and verb. (C) is an unnecessary comma after a question mark. The second comma correctly separates independent clauses connected by a coordinating conjunction.

5. B and C   The clause *he was deeply sorry* should not be set off by commas; it serves as the object (B). The comma between *sorry* and *for* (C) unnecessarily sets off the prepositional phrase. The first comma sets off an introductory phrase.

6.   The colon correctly sets off the explanation for why life "is the greatest bargain." *Life is the greatest bargain: we get it for nothing.*

CHAPTER 3 QUIZ ANSWERS AND EXPLANATIONS *(cont'd)*

7. The two independent clauses are closely related and should be connected by a semicolon. *Doing what you like is freedom; liking what you do is happiness.*

8. These two independent clauses are also closely related and should be separated by a semicolon. *Some people grow under responsibility; others merely swell.*

9. Again, the two independent clauses are closely related and should be connected by a semicolon. A pair of dashes would make the quotation choppy. *Never mind your happiness; do your duty.*

10. The direct quotation should be introduced by a comma and enclosed in quotation marks. The question mark is part of the whole sentence and should be outside the quotation marks. *What did Lindsay mean when she said, "We need to take a break"?*

11. The title of the editorial should be enclosed in quotation marks. The title is essential to the meaning of the sentence so it should not be set off by commas. *The editorial "Justice for Mall" is worth reading.*

12. No correction needed. The dash effectively sets off the introduction from the main clause. The exclamation point suggests that the dash is ideal, indicating emotion.

13. The introductory clause needs to be set off by a comma, but the comma after *see* and the object (the *that* clause) is incorrect. The ratio is correctly expressed by a colon between the numbers. *If you look closely, you will see that the numbers increase at a ratio of 1:3.*

14. B The cat's name *is* UFO—it's not an abbreviation. The error in this sentence is *it's*, the contraction for *it is* (see Chapter 14).

15. A All three of these informal abbreviations should be written out.

16. C None of these sentences are strong enough to warrant an exclamation point. The question mark at the end of the third sentence, a direct question, is correct.

17. D Both of these informal abbreviations should be written out.

CHAPTER 3 QUIZ ANSWERS AND EXPLANATIONS *(cont'd)*

18. E This sentence is correct.

19. B Both *goin* and *fishin* are missing the final *g;* mark this omission with an apostrophe.

20. A Don't use *p.m.* except with a specific time. Don't abbreviate titles unless used with a name.

CHAPTER 4

Spelling, Capitalization, and Italics

BUILDING BLOCK QUIZ

Start with this 10-question Building Block Quiz. The first few questions test material you've already seen.

Determine which underlined portion, if any, contains an error in grammar, mechanics, or style. If there is no error, choose E.

1. I think <u>it's</u> an <u>ingenuous</u> idea, Shashi<u>;</u> however<u>,</u> I don't think
        (A)   (B)   (C)   (D)

    it's very practical. <u>No error</u>
                              (E)

2. <u>Here's</u> an interesting fact for you<u>:</u> more deer are killed by
       (A)   (B)

    drivers each year <u>than</u> by <u>hunter's</u>. <u>No error</u>
                       (C)   (D)   (E)

3. If you think <u>Americans</u> are not wasteful, think again: <u>We</u> use
                     (A)   (B)

    more than 67 million tons of paper each year—that's 580 <u>lbs.</u>
                                                                  (C)

    per person! <u>No error</u>
                     (D)

4. The highest point in Ohio is said to be <u>mount rumpke</u>, a
   (A)

   "<u>mountain</u>" that is really a giant landfill owned by Rumpke,
   (B)

   one of the <u>largest</u> waste and recycling <u>companies</u> in the
                (C)   (D)

   nation. <u>No error</u>
              (E)

5. Steven <u>Siegel's</u> massive sculpture <u>Scale</u> appears at first to be a giant
          (A)   (B)

   block of stone, but it is really <u>composed</u> of 20,000 pounds of
                                     (C)

   <u>recycled</u> newspaper that will eventually begin to degrade. <u>No error</u>
   (D)   (E)

6. Siegel's sculpture is on <u>permanent</u> display at the <u>Sculpture Garden</u>
                            (A)   (B)

   of the Abington <u>art center</u> in Jenkintown, Pennsylvania <u>No error</u>
                   (C)   (D)   (E)

7. <u>Neither</u> option is <u>desireable</u>, but if we have no other choice, <u>then</u>
   (A)   (B)   (C)

   we should take Johnson's <u>advice</u> and reallocate our funds. <u>No error</u>
                            (D)   (E)

8. While many <u>over the counter</u> cold <u>remedies</u> are safe during
              (A)   (B)

   pregnant women should always consult <u>their</u> <u>doctor</u> before taking
                                        (C)   (D)

   any medication. <u>No error</u>
                   (E)

9. Elise is bidding on a <u>coop</u> in the new <u>Myer Building</u> <u>downtown</u>,
                        (A)   (B)   (C)

   but she is <u>worried</u> that she will end up in a bidding war. <u>No error</u>
              (D)   (E)

10. The <u>secretarys</u> in the office have filed a joint complaint <u>alleging</u>
        (A)   (B)

    sexual <u>harassment</u> by several top <u>managers</u> at the firm. <u>No error</u>
             (C)   (D)   (E)

BUILDING BLOCK QUIZ ANSWERS AND EXPLANATIONS

1. B *Ingenious* is the correct word in this context, not *ingenuous*.

2. D *Hunters* should be plural, not possessive; delete the apostrophe.

3. D The informal abbreviation *lbs.* is inappropriate and should be written out.

4. A The proper noun *Mount Rumpke* should be capitalized.

5. B The title of the sculpture *Scale* should be italicized.

6. C The name of a specific place should be capitalized: *Abington Art Center*.

7. B The *e* in *desire* should be dropped when adding a suffix beginning with a vowel.

8. A The words *over the counter* work together to form one modifier for *cold remedies*, so they should be hyphenated: *over-the-counter*.

9. A *Coop* should be hyphenated—*co-op*—to differentiate it from *coop*.

10. A When forming the plural of words ending in –*y*, if the *y* is preceded by a consonant, change the *y* to *ie* before adding –*s*.

SPELLING

English spelling may seem illogical or haphazard, but there are a few powerful rules.

General Rules

Rule 1: *I* before *e* except after *c*, unless the sound is *a* or *i*.

I **before *e*:** relief, achieve, believe, lien, field, chief, mischief, friend, thief

Except after *c*: deceive, conceive, receive

Unless the sound is *a* or *i*: eight, veil, height, weight, neighbor

There are numerous exceptions, including *either and neither* (for those who pronounce those words with a long *e* sound instead of an *i* sound), *counterfeit, caffeine, weird, foreign, seize, protein, skein, leisure, science,* and *conscience.*

Rule 2: Form plurals of most words by adding *–s*.

Add *–es* to nouns ending in *–s, -sh, -ch,* and *–x*. For most nouns ending in *f,* change the *f* to a *v* before adding *–es*.

  letters   foxes   wishes   thieves

Rule 3: Form plurals of hyphenated words by adding the *–s* to the main word.

  editors-in-chief   forget-me-nots

Rule 4: Form plurals of most words derived from foreign languages as they would in their original language.

-um → -a	medium → media
-us → -i	alumnus → alumni
-a → -ae	vertebra → vertebrae
-sis → -ses	hypothesis → hypotheses
-on → -a	criterion → criteria

Rule 5: If a word ends in a silent *–e*, drop the *e* if adding a suffix that begins with a vowel. Keep the *e* if the suffix begins with a consonant.

  live → living, lively   erase → erased, erasure

Exceptions include *argument, truly,* and *changeable.*

Rule 6: If a word ends in *–y* that is preceded by a consonant, change the *y* to *ie* when adding *–s* or *–d*. If the *y* is preceded by a vowel, keep the *y*.

  chutney → chutneys   lily → lilies

Exceptions include proper names ending in *–y* (e.g., *Mahonys*).

Rule 7: If the stress falls on the final syllable and the final vowel is short, double the consonant when adding a suffix beginning with a vowel.

If the consonant is a *c*, use *ck* instead of doubling the *c*.

Double	**Don't Double**
hop → hopped	hope → hoped
fat → fatten	fate → fated
occur → occurrence	label → labeled
panic → panicked	reveal→ revealing

REMEMBER THIS!

Double the final consonant when adding a suffix if the preceding vowel needs to be kept short.

Practice 1

Circle the correct spelling of the word in parentheses in each sentence.

1. These (merry-go-rounds / merries-go-round) were built in the late 1800s.

2. The most important (criteria / criterions) for the award are originality and effectiveness of design.

3. We must remain in the shelter while the flood waters are (recedeing / receding).

Hyphenation

Here are the half-dozen rules for proper hyphen use.

Rule 1: Use hyphens to connect some compound nouns.

Some compound nouns are hyphenated, others are not; some are combined into one word, others stay as two separate words. When in doubt, consult a dictionary.

compound, hyphenated: mother-in-law, cross-examination

compound, one word: roommate, pigtail, sunlight

compound, separate words: test tube, right of way

Rule 2: Use hyphens to connect words functioning together as a modifier.

When two or more words work together to create one modifier for a noun or pronoun that follows them, hyphenate them. Do not use hyphens when they *follow* the noun.

Correct: Charlise is a <u>well-known</u> photographer.

Incorrect: Charlise's photographs are <u>well known</u>.

Rule 3: Hyphenate the prefixes *all-*, *ex-* (when *ex-* means *former*) and *self-*.

Practicing meditation has made me more <u>self-confident</u>.

The team's <u>all-out</u> effort game after game led it to the state championships.

Chloe's <u>ex-boyfriend</u> is still devastated by their breakup.

Most other words formed with prefixes do not have hyphens, except if the second element is capitalized or a number (*anti-Semitic, pre-1800s, mid-May*).

Rule 4: Hyphenate fractions and compound numbers from twenty-one to ninety-nine.

My grandmother turned <u>ninety-five</u> yesterday.

The tank is <u>three-quarters</u> full.

Rule 5: Use hyphens to divide words between syllables at the end of a line.

Divide words *only* between syllables. Don't separate the final syllable unless it is more than two letters.

Rule 6: Use hyphens as needed to avoid ambiguity or separate awkward doubling or tripling of letters.

The <u>re-creation</u> of the accident made it clear who was at fault.

This is a <u>non-negotiable</u> offer.

Practice 2

Insert any necessary hyphens.

4. I made a list of my short and long term goals.

5. Make sure your records are up to date before you register for the fall semester.

6. The movie tells the story of an excon who falls in love with his parole officer.

Practice 3

Indicate with a slash where each word could be divided at the end of a line.

7. egregious

8. microphone

9. stadium

HOMOPHONE MEMORY TIPS

- An arc is curved like a *c*.
- A censor cuts; a sensor sees.
- You hear with your ear.
- All three words in the phrase *whole wide world* begin with *w*.
- The *inn* is crowded because there are two *ns*.
- You peer with your two eyes.
- You add *–s* to form the plural: It's nice to get lots of *presents* on your birthday.
- When you were learning to read, you were *taught* that the *gh* in words like *taught, caught,* and *bought* is silent.

Practice 4

Choose the correct homophone(s) within parentheses.

10. This design is stunning, but I don't think the bridge will be able to (bare / bear) (wait / weight) in the center.

11. If you come over (hear / here) you can (hear / here) the noise clearly.

12. I (kneed / need) to (buy / by / bye) a car by the weekend so I can get to my (knew / new) job on Monday.

A Note About Spell Checkers

If spelling is not your forte, spell checkers in word processing programs can be a tremendous help. But they do *not* eliminate the need for proofreading. Both *fair* and *fare* are spelled correctly, but only one will be correct in context.

Capitalization

Even minor capitalization errors can be disconcerting for readers, so it's important to master these dozen rules.

Rule 1: Capitalize proper nouns.

Proper nouns are the *specific* names of people, places, and things.

Woodrow Wilson	Parker Avenue
Bright Eyes Coffee Company	La Jolla Public Library

Family titles such as *mom* and *dad* should be capitalized only when used as a proper name (as when you directly address that person):

Correct: My <u>mom</u> is going back to college to finish her degree.

Correct: Hey, <u>Mom</u>, are you really going back to college to finish your degree?

Rule 2: Capitalize the first word in a sentence.

This applies to email and other online communications too.

Rule 3: Capitalize the first word of a quoted sentence but not a quoted word or phrase.

> **Capitalize**: To Divjani, "The intensity with which we worship celebrities is profoundly disturbing."
>
> **Don't capitalize**: Divjani is "profoundly disturb[ed]" by the "intensity with which we worship celebrities."

Rule 4: You *may* capitalize the first word after a colon if it begins an independent clause.

But you don't have to. As always, be consistent; capitalize all independent clauses after colons or don't capitalize any.

> **With capital**: Here's my advice: Be honest, but don't share everything.
>
> **Without capital**: Here's my advice: be honest, but don't share everything.

Rule 5: Capitalize abbreviations for organizations, corporations, departments and agencies, and radio and television stations.

> The FBI was founded in 1908; the CIA was created 40 years later in 1947.
>
> The program *Kids Korner* is on WXPN every night at 7:00.
>
> We bought stock in UJB back when the company first started.

Rule 6: Capitalize the first word and all important words in the titles of publications, movies, songs, and works of art.

Do not capitalize prepositions (e.g., *of, for, in*) or articles (*a, the*) except at the beginning of the title.

> Hemingway's novel For Whom the Bell Tolls takes its title from John Donne's poem "Meditation XVII: No Man Is an Island."
>
> My favorite Auguste Rodin sculpture is The Kiss.

Rule 7: Capitalize titles when they precede a name.

> **Capitalize**: Captain Sirico plans to retire at the end of the year.
>
> **Don't capitalize**: Sirico has been a captain for 20 years.

Rule 8: Capitalize the days of the week and months of the year.

The semester ends <u>May</u> 18; I start my internship on the first <u>Tuesday</u> in <u>June</u>.

Rule 9: Capitalize names of specific places and nouns and adjectives derived from them.

I'm a <u>New Yorker</u> through and through.

The <u>Toledo Cathedral</u> in <u>Spain</u> is the most amazing building I've ever seen.

Rule 10: Capitalize the names of special events and historical periods, but not centuries.

The <u>Industrial Revolution</u> began in the late <u>eighteenth century</u> in Great Britain.

The <u>Academy Awards</u> are held in February or March of each year.

Rule 11: Capitalize the names of countries, specific regions, languages, and religions, and adjectives derived from them.

According to the latest census, ninety-five percent of <u>Italians</u> are <u>Roman Catholic</u>.

Rule 12: Capitalize the names of the planets, stars, and other celestial structures.

The <u>Crab Nebula</u>, which is 6000 light years away, is the remnant of a supernova explosion that was visible from <u>Earth</u> in 1054.

What Not to Capitalize

- **Words used for emphasis.** Use italics instead: *never* rather than NEVER.
- The names of **academic subjects** (except languages, specific regions, and specific courses or departments).

  Incorrect: I am majoring in <u>Political Science</u>.

  Correct: My <u>Contemporary Political Science</u> class is fascinating.

- **Seasons**: Tomorrow is the first day of <u>spring</u>.
- The first word of an indirect quotation.

    Incorrect: Hedy told me that <u>She's</u> interested in joining our book group.

    Correct: Hedy told me that <u>she's</u> interested in joining our book group.

Practice 5

Correct any errors in capitalization in the following sentences.

13. Construction on the new Middle School begins next Month.

14. Take your forms to the financial aid office on the Third Floor in the Meyer building.

15. The MacAdoo annual flower and art show is coming up in april.

16. The Officer said, "there's an accident ahead; you'll have to turn around."

ITALICS

Italics—*slanted typeface*—and <u>underlining</u> serve the same functions in writing. Whichever you choose, be consistent. If you can't italicize or underline (e.g., in an email program), enclose the text in asterisks or underscore (e.g., *Looking Ahead* is a fine novel). Here are five rules:

Rule 1: Italicize or underline titles of long or major works.

This includes books, newspapers, magazines, plays, long poems, films, television and radio programs, musical compositions, works of visual or performance art, comic strips, software, and websites.

    This month's *Home Style* magazine has some excellent recipes.

    The author of *American Mania* was recently interviewed on WHYY's *Radio Times*.

    Exceptions: Do not italicize or underline the Bible or books of the Bible, titles of legal documents, or the title of your own paper when writing an essay.

> **FLASHBACK**
>
> Titles of short works or portions of long works (e.g., a poem or chapter in a book) should be enclosed in quotation marks.

Rule 2: Italicize or underline foreign words.

DeeDee's *joie de vivre* is infectious.

Rule 3: Italicize or underline words used specially or (as you've seen in this chapter) letters used as letters.

The right word here is *allusion*, not *illusion*.

Rule 4: Italicize or underline names of ships, trains, aircraft, and spacecraft.

The *Queen Mary II* is the largest cruise ship in the world.

The *Sputnik II* carried the first living creature—a dog—into orbit.

Rule 5: Use italics or underlining to emphasize words or ideas.

As with exclamation points, excessive use of italics or underlining will detract from the emphasis and be distracting.

Ok, but this is the *last time*—I mean it!

Practice 6

Circle any words or phrases that should be italicized or underlined.

17. The Italian word for beautiful is bella.

18. The movie Apollo 13 is the true story of the spacecraft Apollo 13.

19. Oh, Anna, I'm so sorry!

20. Only the contraction they're gets an apostrophe, not their or there.

SUMMARY

General rules for correct **spelling** include:

1. *I* before *e*, except after *c*, unless the sound is *a* or *i*

2. Form the plural of most words by adding –*s*. Form the plural of hyphenated words by adding –*s* to the main word. Form the plural of most words derived from foreign languages as they would in their original language.

3. If a word ends in a silent –*e*, drop the *e* if adding a suffix that begins with a vowel. Keep the *e* if the suffix begins with a consonant.

4. If a word ends in a –*y* preceded by a consonant, change the *y* to *ie* when adding –*s* or –*d*.

5. If the stress falls on the final syllable and the final vowel is short, double a final consonant when adding a suffix beginning with a vowel.

Use a **hyphen**:

1. to connect some compound nouns (check a dictionary)

2. to connect words functioning together as a modifier

3. after the prefixes *all-, ex-* (when it means *former*), and *self-*

4. for fractions and compound numbers up to ninety-nine

5. to divide words between syllables at the end of a line

6. as needed to avoid ambiguity or awkwardness

Be alert for **homophones**.

Most people forget to **capitalize**:

1. the first and all important words in the titles of publications, movies, songs, and artworks

2. titles when they precede a name, but not if they follow a name or stand on their own

3. days of the week and months of the year, but not seasons

4. names of special events and historical periods, but not centuries

5. names of the planets, stars, and other celestial bodies and structures

Use **italics** or **underlining** for:

1. titles of long or major works (e.g., novels, movies, or newspapers)
2. foreign words
3. words used specially or letters used as letters
4. the names of ships, trains, aircraft, and spacecraft
5. to emphasize words or ideas (but only sparingly)

PRACTICE ANSWERS AND EXPLANATIONS

Practice 1

1. merry-go-rounds

2. criteria

3. receding

Practice 2

4. short- , long-term [*short* and *long* both modify *term*]

5. No hyphens. *Up to date* follows the noun it modifies, so it isn't hyphenated.

6. ex-con

Practice 3

7. e/gre/gious

8. mi/cro/phone

9. sta/dium [don't break the 2-letter ending]

Practice 4

10. bear, weight

11. here, hear

12. need, buy, new

PRACTICE ANSWERS AND EXPLANATIONS *(cont'd)*

Practice 5

13. Construction on the new <u>m</u>iddle <u>s</u>chool begins next <u>m</u>onth.

14. Take your forms to the <u>F</u>inancial <u>A</u>id <u>O</u>ffice on the <u>t</u>hird <u>f</u>loor in the Ostermeyer <u>B</u>uilding.

15. The MacAdoo <u>A</u>nnual <u>F</u>lower and <u>A</u>rt <u>S</u>how is coming up in April.

16. The <u>o</u>fficer said, "<u>T</u>here's an accident ahead; you'll have to turn around."

Practice 6

17. The Italian word for <u>beautiful</u> is <u>bella</u>.

18. The movie <u>Apollo 13</u> is the true story of the spacecraft <u>Apollo 13</u>.

19. Oh, Anna, I'm <u>so</u> sorry! [*So* could be italicized for emphasis.]

20. Only the contraction <u>they're</u> gets an apostrophe, not <u>their</u> or <u>there</u>.

CHAPTER 4 QUIZ

Determine which correction, if any, would most improve each sentence.

1. According to Scientists, the typical raindrop falls at the speed of 17 miles per hour.

    (A) Change the capital *s* in *Scientists* to a lower case *s*.

    (B) Change the comma to a colon.

    (C) Change *raindrop* to *rain-drop*.

    (D) Change *miles per hour* to *miles-per-hour*.

    (E) No change

2. Mothers to be crave nachos more than any other food, including ice cream and pickles.

    (A) Change mothers to be to mothers-to-be.

    (B) Capitalize nachos.

    (C) Change nachos to nachoes.

    (D) Change ice cream to ice-cream.

    (E) No change

3. It is officially against the law to burp or sneeze in a Church in Omaha, Nebraska.

    (A) Change against the law to against-the-law.

    (B) Change the capital c in Church to a lower case c.

    (C) Change the capital o in Omaha to a lower case o.

    (D) Change Nebraska to its abbreviation, NE.

    (E) No change

4. The eight year old child has already composed two symphonies that have been critically acclaimed and are being performed by orchestras around the world.

    (A) Change eight year old to eight-year-old.

    (B) Change symphonies to symphonys.

    (C) Change critically acclaimed to critically-acclaimed.

    (D) Change orchestras to orchestra's.

    (E) No change

5. The beauty of the California coastline, especially Big Sur, is unparallelled.

    (A) Capitalize *coastline*.

    (B) Italicize *Big Sur*.

    (C) Capitalize *unparallelled*.

    (D) Change *unparallelled* to *unparalleled*.

    (E) No change

6. Though you doubt my dedication, I am fully committed to seeing this project threw.

   (A) Capitalize *dedication.*

   (B) Change *fully committed* to *fully-committed.*

   (C) Change *committed* to *commited.*

   (D) Change *threw* to *through.*

   (E) No change

7. Dancing is the raison d'etre for Zelda, who has been studying ballet since she was three years old.

   (A) Change dancing to danceing.

   (B) Italicize raison d'etre.

   (C) Italicize ballet.

   (D) Change three years old to three-years-old.

   (E) No change

8. According to *www.hookedonfacts.com*, "there are more nutrients in the Cornflakes package than there are in the Cornflakes."

   (A) Remove the italics from *www.hookedonfacts.com.*

   (B) Capitalize *there.*

   (C) Change *nutrients* to *nutreints.*

   (D) Change *there* to *their.*

   (E) No change

9. After school, we will meet at Zoey's pizza shop to work on our American History project.

   (A) Capitalize *we.*

   (B) Capitalize *pizza shop.*

   (C) Change the capital *H* in *History* to a lower case *h.*

   (D) Capitalize *project.*

   (E) No change

10. I always seem to spell foreign wrong; either I switch the *i* and *e* or forget the *g*.

    (A) Change *foreign* to *foriegn*.

    (B) Italicize *foreign*.

    (C) Capitalize *foreign*.

    (D) Capitalize *i, e,* and *g*.

    (E) No change

11. Tim O'Brien's novel *In The Lake Of The Woods* won the James Fenimore Cooper Prize for historical fiction.

    (A) Capitalize *novel*.

    (B) Remove italics from *In The Lake Of The Woods*.

    (C) Change *In The Lake Of The Woods* to *In the Lake of the Woods*.

    (D) Italicize *James Fenimore Cooper Prize*.

    (E) No change

12. A magician's job is to deceive the members of the audience with slieght of hand.

    (A) Capitalize *magician*.

    (B) Change *deceive* to *decieve*.

    (C) Change *audience* to *audeince*.

    (D) Change *slieght* to *sleight*.

    (E) No change

13. We are two thirds of the way to our goal of $450,000 for the new Greenlawn Children's Library.

    (A) Change two thirds to two-thirds.

    (B) Italicize $450,000.

    (C) Italicize Greenlawn Children's Library.

    (D) Change Children's Library to children's library.

    (E) No change

14. Monica firmly believes her son (who just turned two) will become President of the United States one day.

    (A) Change believes to beleives.

    (B) Change son to sun.

    (C) Change the capital p in President to a lower case p.

    (D) Italicize United States.

    (E) No change

15. Even though Iain is an assistant professor, he is openly antiintellectual and has alienated many of his colleagues.

    (A) Capitalize assistant professor.

    (B) Change assistant professor to assistant-professor.

    (C) Change antiintellectual to anti-intellectual.

    (D) Capitalize colleagues.

    (E) No change

16. Prasaad's play Unamerican has caused quite a stir and has reportedly caught the attention of several major movie studios.

    (A) Italicize *Unamerican*.

    (B) Change *major movie* to *major-movie*.

    (C) Capitalize *movie studios*.

    (D) Change *studios* to *studioes*.

    (E) No change

17. In Guy de Maupassant's short story "The Necklace," Madame Loisel borrows and loses what she believes to be a very valueable necklace.

    (A) Italicize *The Necklace*.

    (B) Change *loses* to *looses*.

    (C) Change *believes* to *beleives*.

    (D) Change *valueable* to *valuable*.

    (E) No change

18. All leaders should remember this quotation by Epicurus: "a man who causes fear cannot be free from fear."

    (A) Change *leaders* to *leader's*.

    (B) Capitalize *leaders*.

    (C) Capitalize *a*.

    (D) Italicize *Epicurus*.

    (E) No change

19. Oliver was extremly disappointed by the reviews of his first novel, but that didn't stop him from writing a second, and third, and fourth...

    (A) Change extremly to extremely.

    (B) Change reviews to reveiws.

    (C) Capitalize novel.

    (D) Change writing to writeing.

    (E) No change

20." *You* are the *only* person in the *whole world* that I can trust!" Xavier exclaimed.

    (A) Delete italics from *you* and *only*.

    (B) Delete all italics.

    (C) Italicize *trust*.

    (D) Put the exclamation point outside the quotation mark.

    (E) No change

CHAPTER 4 QUIZ ANSWERS AND EXPLANATIONS

1. **A** The general noun *scientists* should not be capitalized.

2. **A** *Mothers-to-be* should be hyphenated.

3. **B** The general noun *church* should not be capitalized.

4. **A** *Eight-year-old* is a compound modifier.

CHAPTER 4 QUIZ ANSWERS AND EXPLANATIONS *(cont'd)*

5. D The final *l* shouldn't be doubled; the stress isn't on the final syllable.

6. D *Threw* is the past tense of *throw*; *through* means during the entirety of.

7. B Foreign words should be italicized.

8. B The first word of a full-sentence quotation should be capitalized.

9. B *Pizza shop* is part of the title of the company and should be capitalized.

10. B Words used specially should be italicized.

11. C Except as the first word, prepositions and articles in a title shouldn't be capitalized.

12. D *Sleight* is an exception to the *i* before *e* rule.

13. A Fractions like *two-thirds* should be hyphenated.

14. C Titles should only be capitalized if they precede a name.

15. C Hyphenate *anti-intellectual* to prevent the awkward doubling of the letter *i*.

16. A Titles of major works such as plays should be italicized.

17. D The silent *e* at the end of *value* should be dropped when adding a suffix beginning with a vowel.

18. C Since the quotation is a full sentence, its first word should be capitalized.

19. A The silent *e* at the end of *extreme* should not be dropped when adding a suffix beginning with a consonant.

20. B Use italics for emphasis sparingly; here, the exclamation point is sufficient, though you might italicize *only*.

Diction, Clarity, and Tone

Start with this 10-question Building Block Quiz. The first few questions test material you've already seen.

BUILDING BLOCK QUIZ

Circle **T** for true or **F** for false for each of the following statements.

1. **T F** To make the pronoun *it* a possessive, add an apostrophe and an s.

2. **T F** Use a dash to join two independent clauses.

3. **T F** Adjectives derived from proper names must be capitalized.

4. **T F** *Denotation* is the dictionary meaning of a word.

5. **T F** Use the word *can* when talking about permission, and the word *may* when talking about ability.

6. **T F** *Connotation* can change based on context.

7. **T F** Writers often repeat themselves because if it's worth saying once, it's worth saying again.

8. **T F** Clichés and slang add personality to your writing.

9. **T F** If the reference to a pronoun is unclear, don't use it.

10. **T F** Use "big" words when you can; they add a formal tone that's professional yet approachable.

BUILDING BLOCK ANSWERS AND EXPLANATIONS

1. **False.** An apostrophe is used to create the contraction of *it is*. The possessive form of the pronoun is created with the addition of an s.

2. **False.** Dashes are used to set apart and emphasize parenthetical information, or to highlight something about the items in a list (following the list). Semicolons are used to join two independent clauses.

3. **True.**

4. **True.**

5. **False.** *Can* states ability, and *may* states permission.

6. **True.**

7. **False.** It's better to say it right the first time, and make that the only time. Writers typically repeat themselves when they aren't sure of their message.

8. **False.** Clichés are boring, and should be eliminated. Use fresh images instead. Slang should only be used when you are imitating speech.

9. **True.** Unclear pronoun references can confuse your reader.

10. **False.** "Big" words are pompous and intended to intimidate or impress the reader. Strive instead for a less formal, more comfortable syntax that helps the reader understand your message.

DENOTATION AND CONNOTATION

While writing, you continually make choices about the words you use. It's such an integral part of the process that you probably aren't conscious of it. Most of these choices are a matter of personal preference and an expression of individual style. One writer might describe an event as "incredibly dull" while another might say it was "tedious." If the intended message is conveyed, both choices are valid.

However, there are word choices that can cause problems. In this section, we'll explore the importance of paying attention to denotative and connotative meanings. Using the wrong word, or the right word in the wrong context, can confuse or offend your audience. When you are certain of meaning, and really pay attention to word choice, your writing speaks more clearly.

Denotation

The literal, dictionary meaning of a word is known as its *denotation*. For most of the words you use—like *table*, *costly*, or *special*—the denotative meaning is well known. But *bacchanal*, *koan*, or *salubrious* may need a quick look-up in the dictionary or be left out of your writing. So what is so important about denotation?

Mistakes can occur when you use words you think you're sure of, but you're not. For most writers using a highly complex and ever-evolving language like English, there are thousands of words with meanings that are unclear or unknown. That's not surprising; English includes more than 800,000 words.

What may be surprising is the number of ordinary words and phrases that are often used incorrectly. There are three categories of such words: confused, misused, and substandard. As you read through each category, note those words that cause you trouble.

Confused Words

There are many pairs (and a few trios) of words that look or sound very similar but have meanings that are vastly different. As you study the following list, pay close attention to parts of speech where they are indicated. Many of the confused words have different functions.

accept is a verb meaning *to recognize* or *agree to*; **except** is either a preposition meaning excluding or a conjunction meaning *unless.*

access is a verb meaning *means of approaching*; **excess** is a noun or adjective that means *extra.*

affect is a verb that means *to influence*; **effect** as a noun means *result*; **effect** as a verb means *to bring about (some kind of change).*

all ready is an adjective meaning *completely ready*; **already** is an adverb meaning *previously.*

ascent is a noun meaning *a climb*; **assent** is also a noun, meaning *agreement* and a verb meaning *to agree.*

assure means *to convince (someone)*, **ensure** means *to make certain*; both are verbs.

beside is a preposition meaning *next to*; **besides** is an adverb meaning *in addition to.*

brake means *a device used for slowing or stopping motion*, and *to cause slowing or stopping of motion*; **break** means *an escape* or *the act of separating into parts* and *to separate into parts*; both may be nouns or verbs.

capital is the *city or town that serves as the seat of government*; **capitol** is *a government building.*

cite is a verb meaning *to quote or document*; **sight** is a noun meaning *vision*; site is also a noun, meaning *position* or *place.*

coarse is an adjective meaning *lacking refinement, of rough texture,* or *of inferior quality*; **course** as a noun means *a route of movement*, and as a verb means *to move quickly through.*

complement means *a match* or *to match*; **compliment** means *praise* or *to praise*; both may be nouns or verbs.

continual means *intermittent* or *repeated at intervals*; **continuous** means *without interruption*; both are adjectives.

consul, a noun, means *an official representative of one country who resides in another;* **council** is also a noun, meaning *a group that meets to makes decisions;* **counsel** is a verb that means *to give advice.*

decent, with the accent on the first syllable, is an adjective meaning *well-mannered*; **descent,** with the accent on the second syllable, is a noun meaning *decline or fall.*

disburse means *to pay*, while **disperse** means *to spread out*; both are verbs.

discreet means *prudent* or *trustworthy*; **discrete** means *separate* or *detached*; both are adjectives.

disinterested means *having no strong opinion either way*; **uninterested** means *not caring at all.*

elicit is a verb meaning *to stir up*; **illicit** is an adjective meaning *illegal.*

eminent means *distinguished*, or *high in rank*; **imminent** means *about to happen.*

farther means *beyond*, referring to distance; **further** means *additional*, referring to degree, time, or quantity.

foreword is a noun meaning *an introductory note or preface;* **forward** is an adjective or adverb meaning *toward the front.*

formally is an adverb meaning *in the manner of accepted forms or rules*; **formerly** is also an adverb, meaning *at an earlier time.*

historic refers to what is important in history; **historical** refers to the past in general, regardless of importance.

imply means to *hint* or *suggest*; **infer** means to *conclude based on the evidence provided.*

lay is a transitive verb meaning *the action of placing or putting something somewhere.* **Lie** is intransitive and means *to recline or be placed.* The past tense of *lie* is *lay*, causing more confusion.

miner means *a person who works in a mine*; **minor** is *a person who has not reached the age of majority.*

passed is the past tense of the verb *to pass* and means *went by* or *went away*; **past** is an adjective meaning *over* (as in time) or *ago.*

piece, as a noun, means *a segment of a whole*; as verb, it means *to join together.* **Peace** is a noun meaning *a state of harmony or order.*

personal is an adjective meaning *private* or *individual*; **personnel** is a noun meaning *a group of people employed by a business.*

plain is an adjective meaning *ordinary.* As a verb, **plane** means *to make smooth;* as a noun, it means *a jet* or *a flat surface.*

precede means *to come before*; **proceed** means *to move forward.*

principal, as a noun, means *person in charge*, and as an adjective it means *main*; **principle** means *standard.* **Than** is a conjunction meaning *in contrast to*; **then** is an adverb meaning *next* or *consequently.*

waist is a noun meaning *the part of the body below the ribs and above the hips.* As a noun, **waste** means *refuse*; as a verb, it means *to use carelessly.*

Practice 1

Circle the word that correctly completes the following sentences.

1. I'm not sure what he means because he just (implied, inferred) it.

2. Delia can't stand hockey; she is completely (disinterested, uninterested) in watching with the rest of the party.

3. The English language has many more words (than, then) the French language.

4. After he lost his job, his financial situation was on the (decent, descent).

5. My chicken casserole always earns me (complements, compliments).

Match the following troublesome verbs with their meanings.

6. lie	A. to move (something) up
7. lay	B. to put or place (something)
8. rise	C. to put or place (something)
9. raise	D. to go up
10. sit	E. to rest or recline
11. set	F. to rest

Misused Words

The word pairs in this group look and sound nothing alike, but are frequently misused because their meanings are similar (although not close enough to make them interchangeable).

amount refers to the measurement of things you can't count; **number** refers to the measurement of things you can count

anxious means nervous; **eager** means enthusiastic, or looking forward to something

among is used for comparisons or reference to three or more people or things, **between** for comparisons or reference to two people or things

bring means moving someone or something toward the speaker; **take** means moving someone or something away from the speaker

can states ability, **may** states permission

each other is for situations involving two people or things; **one another** is for situations involving three or more people or things

e.g. is the abbreviation for the Latin "exempli gratia," meaning *free example* or *for example*; **i.e.** is the abbreviation for the Latin "id est," meaning *it is* or *that is*

fewer is used when you can count the items (see "number"), **less** when you cannot count the items (see "amount")

good is an adjective that describes a person, place, or thing; **well** an adverb that describes a verb, an adjective, or adverb; as an adjective, it means **healthy**

more is used for comparisons of two things to each another, **most** for comparisons of one thing to more than one other thing

that is a pronoun that introduces a restrictive (or essential) clause; **which** is a pronoun that introduces a non-restrictive (or unessential) clause

---

REMEMBER THIS!

To remember the difference between *that* and *which*: insert the phrase *by the way* before the phrase or clause following either word. If it makes sense, use *which* (*by the way* indicates that what follows could be left out).

Incorrect: The eggs, which are combined with the milk, make the batter rich.

Correct: The eggs that are combined with the milk make the batter rich.

Practice 2

Can you spot the error? Circle **C** for correct or **I** for incorrect; if incorrect, note the correct word.

12. **C I**   I felt bad when they took the injured player away in the ambulance.

13. **C I**   My professor keeps referring to the Big Three (e.g. Shakespeare, Milton, and Keats), but the class has held much debate on who deserves to be in that group.

14. **C I**   After studying, she did well on the test.

15. **C I**   Can I eat another cookie?

Substandard Words

Your purpose in writing is to convey a message to your readers. If they don't understand what you're saying, you've failed. Reports are intended to share ideas with colleagues and associates. Business communication shouldn't be about impressing the reader with "important-sounding" words, buzzwords, technobabble, or industry-specific jargon. Letters and emails aren't notes to yourself; they should be meaningful to your intended audience.

Many substandard words are used frequently in speech, but are not standard written English and should be avoided. They are only appropriate if you are deliberately imitating someone's speech or adopting a "folksy" tone.

> **REMEMBER THIS!**
>
> Slang, including buzzwords, is inappropriate in most written communications.

acrossed/acrost: a folksy word used incorrectly in place of the adverb and preposition *across*

alot: misspelling of *a lot;* acceptable in informal writing, but not in business or other formal writing

anyways, anywheres: speech dialect form not acceptable in written English; use *anyway* or *anywhere*

brang/brung: used incorrectly as the past tense of *bring*; *brought* is correct

hopefully: incorrect when used as a substitute for "I hope." *Hopefully* is an adverb meaning full of hope.

irregardless: this is a double negative, using the negative prefix *ir-* and suffix *–less*. It is not standard English and should be replaced with *regardless*.

–ize: this overused suffix creates verbs from nouns. Avoid words such as *calendarize*, *potentialize*, and *therapize*.

majorly/minorly: major and minor are adjectives; these substandard forms are attempts to use the words as adverbs.

medias: This Latin word is the plural of *medium*. The alternate plural *mediums* is acceptable.

nowheres/somewheres: see *anywheres*

supposably: often used incorrectly in place of *supposedly*. Only correct when used to mean "capable of being supposed."

theirselves, themself: incorrect forms of *themselves*; because *them* is plural, *self* must be as well; and *their* is the possessive form.

Practice 3

In the following sentences, replace any substandard words with standard ones.

16. The invitation was addressed only to him, but he brang his whole family to the party.

17. We can get into the 9:00 show; supposably they have plenty of tickets left.

18. Walter gets his news from many medias, including radio, television, and newspapers.

Connotation

Although some words may cause confusion, their denotative meanings are straightforward. You can always look up *good* and *well*, for example, to check their definitions. *Connotation* involves emotions, cultural assumptions, and suggestions. For example, you could describe someone who works in a restaurant kitchen as a *chef* or a *cook*. Both words have the same denotation, but *chef* has a more professional connotation.

Connotation can be even more problematic when you consider context. Some words can be used neutrally (that is, without strong positive or negative connotations) in one context, and give strong positive or negative connotation in another context.

Practice 4

Circle the word with the most positive connotation for sentences 19–21.

19. During the kazoo performance, the audience wore (smirks, smiles).

20. He's a very (pushy, aggressive) salesman.

21. In July, we typically get many (humid, sticky) days.

Choose the word with the most negative connotation to fill in the blanks for sentences 22–24.

22. Hearing the fire alarm ringing, he (walked, ambled) out of the building.

23. Not only was it rainy in London, but it was (breezy, blustery) as well.

24. The crowd outside the auditorium was (loud, cacophonous).

BIASED LANGUAGE OR INCLUSIVE LANGUAGE

Connotations change with the passage of time. Consider the term *administrative assistant,* which is the title we currently give to an employee who assists another with clerical duties. A few decades ago, that person was a *secretary,* but that term took on a negative connotation and was replaced. There are now signs that *administrative assistant* will meet the same fate. The day set aside to honor these workers is *Administrative Professionals'* Day.

Other words and phrases that have taken on negative connotations over time involve gender, racial and ethnic identity, and physical ability. At one time, the term *handicapped* was considered neutral. When some found it offensive, that word was replaced with *disabled*, which in turn gave way to *differently abled* or *physically challenged*.

If you are not aware of these types of connotations, your writing may be considered biased. Stereotypes and other hurtful or offensive language alienate you from your audience, and obscure the real meaning of your communication. How can you avoid biased language and make your writing more inclusive? Here are some rules:

> **SHARP WRITING TIP**
>
> If you're guilty or unaware of biased writing, take notes.

Gender

Avoid the exclusive use of masculine pronouns by rewriting sentences to eliminate the need for any pronoun; using *he/she*, and *him/her* (but don't overuse these); alternating between masculine and feminine; or making the pronoun and its antecedent plural (*them* and *they* are gender neutral).

Incorrect: Any commuter wishing to buy a ticket should have his money ready.

Correct: Any commuter wishing to buy a ticket should have money ready.

Correct: Commuters wishing to buy tickets should have their money ready.

Use titles that avoid overstressing gender. *Chairperson* (or just *chair*) is preferable to *chairman* or *chairwoman*. *Businessperson* or *executive* is better than *businessman*.

Incorrect: The congressmen discussed the bill in the elevator.

Correct: The members of Congress discussed the bill in the elevator.

Racial and Ethnic Identity

Leave out references to race and ethnicity unless specifically needed. If you do mention a race or ethnic group, use the words preferred by that group. For example, *Asian* and *Native American* are acceptable, while the once favored *Oriental* and *Indian* are not.

Incorrect: How many Oriental students are enrolled in the University?

Correct: How many Asian students are enrolled in the University?

Physical Ability

As with race and ethnicity, do not mention physical ability unless necessary. If you must use labels, use those that are preferred, such as *disabled* and *disability* rather than *crippled* and *handicap*. Question your use of phrases such as *suffering from*, *victim of*, and *confined to*.

Incorrect: Blind singer Andrea Bocelli performed.

Incorrect: Her math teacher is dying of cancer.

Correct: Singer Andrea Bocelli performed in a concert.

Correct: Her math teacher is living with cancer.

Practice 5

Replace biased language in the following sentences with more inclusive words and phrases.

25. Ask the stewardess to get you another cup of coffee.

26. My brave boss, who is the victim of leukemia, ran the meeting last Tuesday.

27. African-American Aretha Franklin is my favorite singers.

CLARITY AND CONCISION

Words such as *sleep*, *slumber*, *rest*, and *repose* vary in shade. They provide writers with the opportunity to say exactly what they mean. Why, then, is so much of what we read confusing or boring? By choosing the word that is exactly right, you convey your message in as few words as possible. Don't use ten words when three will do.

Here are three points to keep in mind.

Don't repeat yourself

This one seems simple, but is seen too often, in too many types of writing, to ignore. Repetition typically occurs when writers aren't sure of exactly what they want to say. They end up with paragraphs or pages of "variations on a theme" that can put the most ardent reader to sleep.

> What I mean to say is, I think our department should probably set some goals. We've been working too hard, for too long, without something specific to aim for. We're all going off in different directions. Why don't we sit down together, have a meeting, and decide where we want to be six months from now? Let's plan for the future and set some goals so we can all work toward them together.

Not only does this use five sentences to say repeatedly what was already said in one or two, but it also sounds less than professional.

> Everyone in our department has been working in a different direction without a specific target. Let's have a meeting to set some goals and work together to achieve them.

These two sentences are confident and professional. They convey the message without repetition. The reader knows exactly what the writer means, and no time has been wasted.

Economize

After you eliminate repetition of ideas, look at your words. Some writers use too many words because they think it sounds more important or intelligent. But wordiness has the opposite effect. Economy can be as simple as deleting extraneous words and phrases.

> It has been indicated that there will be a snowstorm tonight.

What purpose does the introductory phrase serve? If it's important to know who predicted the storm, this sentence fails because it doesn't identify the forecaster. You can also tighten your writing by eliminating redundant parts of a phrase.

Words and phrases that often function as extraneous padding include:

a lot of	(replace with *many* or *much*)
all of a sudden	(replace with *suddenly*)
are able to	(replace with *can*)
as a matter of fact	(delete)
as the case may be	(delete)
basic necessity	(delete *basic*)
basically	(consider deleting)
by and large	(delete)
compare and contrast	(delete either one)
completely finish	(delete *completely*)
continue on	(delete *on*)
due to the fact that	(replace with *because*)
extremely	(consider deleting)
final destination	(delete *final*)
for all intents and purposes	(delete)
in order to	(delete *in order*)
in the event that	(replace with *if*)
in the near future	(replace with *soon*)
initial preparation	(delete *initial*)
on a daily basis	(replace with *daily*)
period of time	(delete *period of*)
personal opinion	(delete *personal*)
progress forward	(delete *forward*)
quite	(consider deleting)
somewhere in the neighborhood of	(replace with *about*)
split apart	(delete *apart*)
the reason why	(delete *the reason*)
through the use of	(delete *the use of*)
totally obvious	(delete *totally*)
very	(consider deleting)
with regard to	(replace with *regarding*)

> **REMEMBER THIS!**
> Never use two words when one will do.

Practice 6

In the following sentences, cross out extraneous and repetitious words and phrases.

28. During the period of time in question, each and every man, woman, and child was able to receive a hot meal last week.

29. Thanks to true and accurate reporting, the story about the space crew not reaching its final destination was revealed to the public.

30. It was totally obvious that every car that is black in color, when you compare and contrast them with cars that are lighter in color, get dirty faster.

31. For all intents and purposes, the meeting that was held with our biggest client was a complete and utter failure.

DON'T BE AMBIGUOUS

Some of the lessons you learned in chapters 1–3 will help you write more precisely. Let's revisit four of them.

Pronoun references must be clear.

If it's not obvious to whom or what they refer, eliminate the pronouns.

Incorrect: Parents agree they show too much violence on TV. (Who are "they"?)

Incorrect: Graduation is coming soon, which is nice. (What does which refer to?)

Dangling or misplaced modifiers should be corrected.

Modifiers work best when they are near the word or words they modify. What is meant:

I nearly scared everyone on the boat.

OR

I scared nearly everyone on the boat.

Use the active voice.

The active voice forces you to focus on both the action and its performer.

Incorrect: A decision was reached to close the factory.

Correct: The board of directors decided to close the factory.

Use precise words.

Why just hint at your intended meaning? Business writing in particular calls for details. Instead of *there is a meeting this afternoon,* write *there is a meeting today at 2:00,* or better yet *the managers will meet today at 2:00. Our financial goals for the year have been met* is clearer than *financially, we're doing well.*

Vague or understated writing is dull. Get specific and don't settle for meaningless clichés. Consider these examples, noting that the more specific or emotional language will not clutter or add unnecessary words.

Succinct:	Vague:
Productive	Much was accomplished
On Tuesday	In a few days
November 15th	Soon
Elated	Happy
Earned us $___	Was profitable
A week late	somewhat behind schedule
Slump	hard economic times
Skyrocket	go up high
Overflow crowd	many people
85 miles an hour	fast

Practice 7

Replace vague words and phrases, if any, with more concrete language. Make up details as necessary.

32. This computer is really expensive.

33. Because of some unforeseen problems we are having, we will

    not be able to fill your order for a while.

34. Her career is going well.

35. He liked the gift he was given.

For each of the following sentences, identify the specific problem that creates wordiness in the sentence. Choose from the following list:

a. imprecise language

b. intensifiers or wishy-washy language

c. passive voice

d. lack of action verb

e. it is/there is construction

f. clause or phrase that could be a modifier

g. clutter word(s) or phrase(s)

h. unnecessary repetition

___36. Sputnik I, the first man-made satellite to orbit the Earth, was only about as small in size as a soccer ball.

___37. Neptune is orbited by at least 13 moons.

___38. Francis's accident is what made me realize that I shouldn't take anything for granted.

___39. This gun has the appearance of having been recently shot, said the detective.

___40. The CD disk player is broken.

41. Revise the following letter to eliminate wordiness.

Dear Mr. Pritchard:

The reason I am writing to you is because I want to complain about the way I was treated by one of your employees.

On Tuesday I had a very strange and weird experience while shopping at your store. As I was carefully looking over your produce, one of your employees began to start stacking fruit next to me. When I looked over to see what he was doing, he stopped.

After he stopped he looked at me and said, "Nanoo nanoo." Then he stood there and looked hard at me for a long time without saying a word, until the point at which I walked away. As I was leaving he said again, "Nanoo nanoo."

This employee was about 5'10" tall in height. He had wavy black hair down to his shoulders. He wore thick glasses. The glasses were tortoise shell and large.

It should be clear to see that this employee made me feel very funny. I do not wish to return back to your store to have another experience like that again.

Sincerely,

Herbert Haines

Revise the following sentences to eliminate any ambiguity or vagueness.

42. *Headline*: Two Boats Collide, One Dies

43. We covered the wall with cracks.

44. I convinced her dogs are too much work to make good pets.

45. The divers said when there are sharks they are not scared of them.

46. After months at sea dreaming of a better life, the Statue of Liberty finally appeared on the horizon.

47. Revise the following paragraph to add variety in sentence structure.

Stanley Kubrick directed *Dr. Strangelove*. It was released in 1964. It is a classic satire about nuclear war. Kubrick wrote the screenplay. The screenplay is based on a novel by Peter George. A rogue general tries to initiate a nuclear attack on Russia. The problem is both countries have enough nuclear weapons to destroy each other. An attack by one side meant a counter-attack by the other. An attack would thus violate the military doctrine of MAD. MAD stands for Mutually Assured Destruction. MAD was supposed to prevent nuclear war.

TONE AND VOICE

Tone and voice convey attitude, individuality, and energy, making your message something that's worth reading. Note that in this context, *voice* refers not to verb forms (active or passive), but to the personal qualities of writing. Just as your speaking voice is unique, so is your writing voice.

Tone

Tone is the attitude you express toward your audience and your subject by your word choice, sentence and paragraph structure, and punctuation. It ranges on a sliding scale:

Formal..........	Informal
Serious..........	Humorous
Pompous..........	Friendly
Heavy..........	Light
Impersonal..........	Personal

We are going to the café to have coffee and discuss politics.

We're going to hang out at the café, have some joe, and chat about politics.

What is the tone of these sentences? Their meaning is nearly identical, but they convey it very differently. The first is straightforward without being overly formal or informal. Consider the word "discuss." It could have been the more formal *converse*, or the less formal *chat*. The second sentence uses chat, along with the slangy "joe" and the contraction "we're." It is very casual.

To determine the appropriate level of formality, you need to consider three aspects of every writing task: your (1) subject, (2) audience, and (3) purpose. Specifically, four questions to ask are: (1) What sort of style does your subject deserve? (2) Who is your audience? (3) What is your relationship to the audience? and (4) What style best fits your purpose?

Tone helps your reader feel comfortable about what you're saying. If you wrote the second sentence to elderly relatives, would it make them comfortable, conveying the message that you are interested in communicating? Would they understand you? Keep your audience in mind, and write using a tone that will work for them.

Voice

With voice, your reader hears *you* in your writing. You are the one who chose to say *antidote* instead of *cure*. You used short sentences to make a point and create a rhythm, or you used longer, more complex sentences to indicate the importance of your topic. Your voice is your writing style. It's how you use all of the information packed into the first four chapters of this book.

Of course, you still need to keep audience in mind, tempering or modulating voice to fit the occasion. An email to a friend should sound very different than an English Lit paper or a report for your boss. But your style should be present in all communications. You never need to sound mechanical, whether writing academic papers or business memos.

> **REMEMBER THIS!**
>
> When you must adopt a formal tone, your voice should be a whisper. Formality expresses concern for the subject and respect for the audience.

What does writing look like without voice? Here is the first paragraph of an emailed meeting synopsis sent to all in attendance.

> Yesterday, there was a discussion of current client supply problems followed by lunch and a strategy session in Conference Room A. All employees were in attendance. The executive in charge of the account, Peter Larou, gave his analysis of the situation. He explained key areas in which improvements should be made, and detailed those improvements. He then proceeded to field questions and comments from others, and many useful suggestions were made. It was productive.

To improve this, consider the audience. The author is writing to her colleagues, all of whom were at the meeting, so why give details they already know (that everyone was there and where the meeting was)? The important information—the suggested improvements—isn't in the paragraph. Business people receive dozens of emails a day; be respectful of their time by quickly giving them the information they need.

> **SHARP WRITING TIP**
>
> Adjust tone, voice, and content for audience.

Then consider tone. Writing to colleagues doesn't require such a formal tone, but extreme informality wouldn't be appropriate either. It should be formal enough to show that the content is serious, but informal enough to engage the audience: probably using "you," and even including a contraction or two. Here is the same email with more voice:

> Thank you for attending and participating in the very productive discussion yesterday. We all came away with a greater understanding of the client supply problems we face, and how to address them. Here's a summary of the points agreed upon during the strategy session.

If your writing suffers from lack of voice, try one or more of these methods:

- Explore and express your thoughts and feeling about the topic.
- Picture your readers and "talk" to them through your writing.
- Use the active rather than the passive voice.
- Don't be pompous; being direct and concise is better than trying to impress.
- Read your words aloud; if they sound wooden they probably don't belong.
- Read it aloud to someone you trust, and ask if it sounds like you.
- Be confident. If your subject is intimidating, do more research. If the writing process is intimidating, write more! Keep a journal or blog, correspond with friends and family.

> **SHARP WRITING TIP**
>
> Use techniques for injecting voice into writing.

Practice 8

Choose the response that best describes each sentence.

48. Let's have a meeting to talk about whether we should take on new clients right now.

    (A) Tone is informal.

    (B) Sounds wooden—needs voice.

    (C) Audience is not considered.

    (D) Tone is too formal for an email.

49. It might be a good idea to talk about whether or not we are too busy to take on new clients right now, but maybe not.

    (A) Tone is humorous.

    (B) Voice is too serious.

    (C) Voice is not confident.

    (D) Audience should be addressed directly.

50. Just when you thought we had too much work, we've got new clients knocking on the door! Should we let them in and start working 80 hours a week?

    (A) Humorous voice works well.

    (B) Good use of less formal word choices.

    (C) Formality level fits audience.

    (D) Tone is too informal.

SUMMARY

Style is about the words you use and how you use them. The style of great writers makes their writing come alive, communicating clearly and correctly without boring or annoying them.

Denotation refers to the dictionary meaning of a word. Because many of the words in our language are often confused or misused, it's important to understand denotation to make better choices.

Connotation is a word's implied meaning, which can change based on context: you could say that a train *departed*, but using that word at a funeral means something very different. Connotations also change over time: words that were once acceptable are now considered offensive. Be particularly mindful of connotation when writing about gender, race and ethnic identity, and physical ability.

Concision is about using as few words as possible to get your point across. Choose the precise words needed. Eliminate ambiguous and meaningless words and phrases. Don't use a phrase when a word will do, don't use a clause when a phrase will do, and don't use a sentence when a clause will do.

Clarity means saying precisely what you mean. Check your writing for pronoun or modifier ambiguity. Don't be vague when you can be specific.

Tone is the attitude you take toward your audience and your subject. You convey tone through word choice, sentence and paragraph structure, and punctuation. It may be formal or casual, serious or humorous, positive or negative. Consider who your readers are, and use a tone that will make them feel comfortable.

Voice should be allowed to come through in your writing to make it lively and personable. Voice is confident without trying to impress. It speaks to the audience in a friendly but intelligent way.

PRACTICE ANSWERS AND EXPLANATIONS

Practice 1

1. *implied,* which means to hint at

2. *uninterested; disinterested* means not having an opinion, which is not the case if you can't stand something

3. *than,* which means in contrast to

4. *descent;* a noun is called for, and *decent* is an adjective

5. *compliments,* which means praise

6. E

7. C

8. D

9. A

10. F

11. B

Practice 2

12. **Correct;** the speaker is referring to emotional feelings.

13. **Incorrect;** the speaker means to say "*that is,*" (*i.e.*). The writers in the parentheses are not examples of the Big Three—they are the Big Three.

14. **Correct;** the adverb *well* modifies the verb *did.*

15. **Incorrect;** the speaker is probably physically capable of eating—he or she is asking permission, so *may* should be used.

PRACTICE ANSWERS AND EXPLANATIONS *(cont'd)*

Practice 3

16. **Incorrect***; brang* is not the correct past tense form; it should be changed to *brought.*

17. **Incorrect***; supposably* is incorrect; use *supposedly* instead.

18. **Incorrect***; medias* is not the correct plural form; it should be *mediums* or *media.*

Practice 4

19. *smiles; smirks* connotes a more negative reaction

20. *aggressive; pushy* connotes rude and obnoxious behavior

21. *humid; sticky* sounds more unpleasant that mere humidity

22. *ambled;* most people leave a building that may be on fire more quickly than what *ambling* connotes

23. *blustery;* this word connotes more severe weather than *breezy*

24. *cacophonous; loud* refers just to volume, while *cacophonous* connotes both volume and unpleasant types of sounds

Practice 5

Note that there are acceptable variations to these responses.

25. Ask the flight attendant to get you another cup of coffee.

26. My boss ran the meeting last Tuesday.

27. Singer Aretha Franklin is one of my favorites.

Practice 6

Answers may vary. Check to see if you eliminated wordiness and repetition.

28. Last week, everybody received a hot meal.

29. Thanks to accurate reporting, the public heard the story about the space crew not reaching its destination.

PRACTICE ANSWERS AND EXPLANATIONS *(cont'd)*

30. It is obvious that, in comparison with lighter colored cars, black cars get dirty faster.

31. The meeting with our biggest client was a complete failure.

Practice 7

Answers will vary. Check to see that you have replaced the vague language with more precise words and phrases.

32. The IBM NetVista costs $1,200.

33. Because one of our manufacturing machines is broken and awaiting repair, we will not be able to fill your order until the 20th.

34. She was promoted for the third time.

35. He was thrilled with the sweater from his girlfriend.

36. **h**

37. **c**

38. **d**

39. **c**

40. **h**

41. Answers will vary, because there is much wrong with this letter and many ways to revise to make the letter more concise. Notice how this revision eliminates clutter and repetition, combines sentences and simplifies structure, and uses more precise words.

Dear Mr. Pritchard:

I am writing to complain about the way I was treated by one of your employees on Tuesday.

PRACTICE ANSWERS AND EXPLANATIONS *(cont'd)*

As I was examining your produce, an employee began stacking fruit next to me. When I looked over to see what he was doing, he stopped, looked at me, and said, "Nanoo nanoo." Then he stared silently at me for a minute until I walked away. As I was leaving, he repeated, "Nanoo nanoo."

This employee was about 5'10" tall with wavy black hair down to his shoulders. He wore large, thick tortoise-shell glasses.

You can imagine that this employee made me very uncomfortable. I do not wish to return to your store to have a similar experience.

Sincerely,

Herbert Haines

Answers will vary. We've underlined our changes to each sentence below.

42. Two Boats Collide; One <u>Person</u> Dies

43. We covered the wall <u>that had</u> cracks.

44. I convinced her <u>that</u> dogs are too much work to make good pets.

45. The divers said <u>they are not afraid when there are sharks around them.</u>

46. After months at sea dreaming of a better life, <u>Yvgeny finally saw the Statue of Liberty appear on the horizon.</u>

47. Answers will vary. Note how we turned some simple sentences into modifiers and varying sentence openers.

Stanley Kubrick's 1964 classic *Dr. Strangelove* is a biting satire about nuclear war based on a novel by Peter George. In Kubrick's screenplay, a rogue general tries to initiate a nuclear attack on Russia. The problem is both countries have enough nuclear weapons to destroy each other; an attack by one side meant a counter-attack by the other. An attack would violate the military doctrine of MAD, or Mutually Assured Destruction, which was supposed to prevent nuclear war.

Practice 8

48. **a.** The contraction *let's* and pronoun *we*, along with words choices like *talk about* rather than *discuss*, and *take on* rather than the more formal *accept*, make the tone informal.

49. **c.** No matter what you're writing about (even if you're writing to say you don't understand something), your voice should be confident. Using modifying phrases such as *might be a good idea* and *but maybe not* tells your reader not to take you seriously.

50. **d.** This example is too informal even for the closest business colleagues. The tone borders on sarcasm, which is inappropriate for the subject.

CHAPTER 5 QUIZ

If necessary, correct the underlined word or words.

1. <u>Lie</u> that book down next to the lamp.

2. She would never tell your secret; she's too <u>discrete.</u>

3. I <u>feel bad</u> that you won't be able to come swimming with us.

4. Rafael's dog won't go <u>anywheres</u> without him.

5. <u>Denotation</u> involves the cultural assumptions placed on words.

6. <u>Blind</u> has a more positive connotation than <u>visually impaired</u>.

7. Ask the <u>stewardess</u> to bring you another cup of coffee.

8. Use gender-neutral titles to avoid <u>biased</u> language.

9. Repeating ideas in your writing can make you sound <u>more</u> professional and get your message across better.

10. <u>Considering the fact that</u> <u>each and every</u> man on the team is <u>tired and exhausted,</u> we should end the press conference <u>at this time</u>.

11. Genie, Nancy, and I are going shopping in <u>her</u> car.

12. <u>Thinking ahead</u>, I'm not sure that taking out a home equity loan is such as good idea. Interest rates could go up.

13. <u>A decision was made.</u>

14. Many <u>clarity</u> problems are caused by misplaced and dangling modifiers.

15. Tone refers to the attitude expressed in your writing; it could be serious or <u>heavy</u>, formal or informal, impersonal or personal.

16. All employees are asked to please refrain from posting incendiary messages, downloading suspicious programs, visiting nefarious Web sites, and <u>slopping down greasy lunches</u> over the keyboard!

17. Use tone to put your <u>audience</u> at ease.

18. Reading your writing <u>to yourself</u> is a good way to check for voice.

19. The addition of contractions can make your writing <u>more</u> formal.

20. Awareness of your audience <u>can make it difficult</u> to establish the right tone and voice.

CHAPTER 5 QUIZ ANSWERS AND EXPLANATIONS

1. Change to *lay*. *Lie* means "to recline," *lay* means "to put or place something down" and takes an object.

2. Change to *discreet*. *Discrete* mean "separate."

3. **Correct.** *Feel bad* refers to emotional feelings. "Feel badly" might mean some of the nerve endings are malfunctioning.

4. Change to *anywhere*. *Anywheres* is not considered part of standard written English.

5. Change to *connotation*. *Denotation* refers to the dictionary definition.

6. Switch the underlined terms. *Blind* has a less positive connotation than *visually impaired*.

7. Change to *flight attendant*. Words such as *stewardess* are considered biased.

8. **Correct.** *Chairperson* and *weather forecaster* are preferable to *chairman* and *weatherman*.

9. Change to *less*. Repetition can bore your reader, and make you sound unsure of your message.

10. *Considering the fact that* should be replaced with *because*. Either *each* or *every* should be removed. Either *tired* or *exhausted* should be removed. *At this time* should be replaced with *now*.

11. Change to *Genie's or Nancy's*. The pronoun reference is unclear.

12. **Correct.** The phrase *thinking ahead* clearly modifies the subject of the sentence, *I*.

13. Rewrite in the active voice, adding information. Who made the decision, and what was it?

14. **Correct.**

15. Change to an antonym of *heavy*, such as *light* or *humorous*.

CHAPTER 5 QUIZ ANSWERS AND EXPLANATIONS cont'd

16. Change to a phrase that repeats the idea, but in a more formal tone that fits with the rest of the sentence. An example is, *eating over the keyboard.*

17. **Correct.**

18. Change to *aloud.*

19. Change to *less.* Contractions, personal pronouns, and less formal word choices (*chew* instead of *masticate*) make your writing less formal.

20. Change to *makes it easier to.* When you know who your readers are, you can gauge level of formality, word choices, and other components of tone and voice.

SECTION II
Sharper Writing Stages

Prewriting

BUILDING BLOCK QUIZ

Identify the part of speech (function) of each underlined word in sentences 1–5. Identify **subject and object, verb tenses, pronoun forms, and conjunction types**.

1. <u>Snowboarding</u> can trace its roots to the 1920s, <u>when</u> children created makeshift snowboards from barrel staves and plywood.

2. In 1965, an engineer invented the <u>Snurfer</u> (snow surfer) that was marketed as a children's toy; a few years later, over half a million <u>had sold</u>.

3. <u>One</u> fan of the Snurfer was <u>Vermonter</u> Jake Burton.

4. Burton began making snowboards; <u>they</u> were <u>typically</u> made out of wood with rubber straps as bindings.

5. The sport's popularity <u>grew</u> during the 1980s, as <u>seasoned skiers and youngsters new to the slopes</u> embraced it.

Circle **C** for correct for those sentences with no grammatical errors, and **I** for incorrect for those with errors. Responses of I should also include the type of error.

6. **C I** Good journalists who perform thorough research.

   Error types:_____

7. **C I** Interviewing her subject, the tape recorder broke.

   Error types:_____

8. **C I** She got her subject to open up when she asks neutral questions and takes the time to listen.

   Error types:_____

9. **C I** The article was written by the reporter.

   Error types:_____

10. **C I** Either our local paper or the regional one followed the story.

   Error types:_____

Correct the errors (if any) in the following sentences.

11. Its a great opporotunity for the class of 04, they get to lead

    the Class Song at our reunion.

12. A rowsing sing-along will help deemphasize the fact that the

    reunion is not well-attended.

13. The president of the university is scheduled to give a speach after

    we hear from the Board of Trustees.

14. The Homeowner's Association is sponsoring a lecture by Herbert

    Dickinson MD.

15. After the movie let's head downtown, everyone will be hungry for

    supper.

16. Ask the stewardess to bring more peanuts to each and every

    member of our group.

17. Due to the fact that his actionable report urges us to progress

    forward, I think we should follow it.

Circle the correct word to complete each sentence.

18. Would you hand me the lid (that/which) fits on this pot?

19. (Disperse, Disburse) the funds (irregardless/regardless) of (their, they're) plan.

20. (Can, May) I choose (among/between) the three available options?

BUILDING BLOCK ANSWERS AND EXPLANATIONS

1. *Snowboarding* is a gerund (a verb form that acts as a noun) functioning as the subject of the sentence. *When* is a subordinating conjunction (a conjunctive adverb, it introduces a subordinate clause).

2. *Snurfer* is a noun functioning as the object of the verb *invented. Had sold* is a verb in the past perfect tense.

3. *One* is an adjective that describes the noun *fan. Vermonter* is a noun functioning as an adjective (it modifies the noun *Jake Burton*).

4. *They* is a plural pronoun that replaces the noun *snowboards. Typically* is an adverb that describes the verb *made.*

5. *Grew* is an intransitive verb (it has no object). *Seasoned skiers and youngsters new to the slopes* is a compound subject.

6. **Incorrect**; sentence fragment. There is a subject (*journalists*), but no verb. The clause *who perform thorough research* is a subordinate clause.

BUILDING BLOCK ANSWERS AND EXPLANATIONS *(cont'd)*

7. **Incorrect**; dangling modifier. *Interviewing her subject* has nothing to modify, because the subject of the sentence is *the tape recorder* (which could not conduct an interview).

8. **Incorrect**; unnecessary shift. The sentence begins with the past tense (*got her subject*), and changes to the present (*asks, takes*).

9. **Incorrect**; inappropriate use of the passive voice.

10. **Correct**.

11. *Its* should be *It's* (contraction of *it is*); *opporotunity* is spelled *opportunity*; *04* should be *'04*; *class song* should not be capitalized.

12. *Rowsing* is spelled *rousing*; *deemphasize* needs a hyphen (*de-emphasize*); *well attended* does not need a hyphen.

13. *President* should be capitalized; *speach* is spelled *speech*.

14. The apostrophe in *homeowners* should follow the *s*; a comma should set off the title *MD*.

15. A comma should follow the introductory phrase *after the movie*; a semicolon rather than a comma should separate the closely related independent clauses (*let's head downtown* and *everyone will be hungry for supper*).

16. *Stewardess* should be replaced with the gender-neutral *flight attendant*; *each and every* is redundant, so one of the words should be eliminated.

17. *Due to the fact* that is wordy, so replace it with the more concise *because*; *actionable* is a business buzzword and not standard English, so it should be eliminated or replaced with an adjective that describes the report; *progress forward* is redundant and should be simply *progress*.

18. *That*; the clause *that fits on this pot* is essential, because it determines the lid to be chosen.

19. The correct word, *disburse,* means *to pay* (*disperse* means *to spread out*); *irregardless* is not standard English; *their* is the possessive pronoun (*they're* is a contraction of *they are*).

20. *May*, which indicates permission as opposed to ability; *among*, because *between* refers to just two people or things.

THE WRITING PROCESS

The following three chapters examine the writing process step by step. First you'll learn how to get ideas on paper and organize them using a variety of prewriting strategies. In chapter 6 you'll see how a well thought-out plan is executed, becoming a piece of writing. Chapter 7 will explain the art of fine-tuning. Revising, editing, and proofreading will polish your work and leave the mistakes behind.

The strategies in this chapter represent the first two stages of the writing process. In the first stage, you formulate ideas. Whether your topic is clear, or you're not sure what you want to say, there is a technique that can assist you in putting workable ideas on paper. The second stage involves planning your writing by organizing the material you gathered in the first stage.

All of these strategies are offered as suggestions. Some writers prefer one or two, and use them for any type of writing they tackle, whether personal, business, or academic. Others use different strategies for different writing forms. Work your way through the entire chapter. To familiarize yourself with all of them, even if a strategy hasn't worked for you in the past, read over the material and do the practice activities. Presented differently, the technique may work well for you now.

STAGE 1: GETTING IDEAS ON PAPER

The five strategies in this stage will help you move from "I don't know where to begin" to developing workable ideas for your writing. They're not all suitable for every type of writing situation you'll encounter, so learn them all, and be prepared to prewrite no matter what type of final product you're after.

Brainstorming

What It Is

Brainstorming is an active, energetic method of getting your ideas on paper. In order to brainstorm effectively, you must first establish a topic. If your writing is an assignment, you've already got an idea about which direction you'll take. If your boss has asked you to write a report, you know, at least generally, the material you need to cover. The idea behind brainstorming is that, even if you feel hesitant or nervous about tackling your topic, chances are you've already got some good ideas about how to approach it. You just need to get them from your brain onto the page.

Getting It Right

To begin, write your topic at the top of a blank piece of paper. Then, let go. Write down any and every thought that comes to mind pertaining to that topic (remember the word *brainstorm* contains the word *storm*!) Try not to edit yourself yet; you can always toss out an idea later if it doesn't make sense, or doesn't fit with the topic. Don't worry about spelling or grammar.

You might write ideas in a list, in short phrases, or as a "web," with lines drawn between connecting ideas. It doesn't matter how you put the information on paper, as long as you understand what your notations mean. Don't get bogged down in details, which can slow the process. If you know you'll need specific information later, make a note of it. And remember that your brainstorming will be impossible to use if you can't read it; neatness doesn't count, but legibility does!

Example

Suppose you need to write a proposal that argues for updating your company's safety regulations regarding winter weather conditions. You'll probably have to do some research during the writing process to fill in such details as key dates, federal regulations, and safety violations. But, as our following sample shows, brainstorming merely mentions those things, and moves on.

> improve training for workers
> check OSHA website for compliance issues
> improve company's safety record—list past problems
> cold weather injuries: detail each one

how to better treat injuries (train staff)

teach warning signs for hypothermia

mandatory breaks in heated trailer

issue of clothing—should we provide?

Workers w/ existing medical conditions—screening for

Provide warm beverages at all work sites

Why It's Effective

Our example lists at least ten distinct ideas. Some are very specific, while others are general and will need further clarification. There are questions that require thought and investigation, and prompts for the writer to perform research. It's important to allow this kind of diversity in brainstorming. Don't limit yourself to a list of similar ideas, or try to find a link between them.

SHARP WRITING TIP

Don't edit while brainstorming; list as many distinct and diverse ideas as you can come up with.

Practice 1

Choose one of the following topics. Brainstorm on it for three minutes on your own paper.

(A)   Why I enjoy my favorite books

(B)   Where I would like to live

(C)   How I handle anger

(D)   How to describe a rose to an alien

Freewriting

What It Is

Freewriting is similar to brainstorming in that you write ideas as they come to mind without editing.

But freewriting differs in that it is best used when you don't have a specific topic. If you need to write an essay, but have been given the freedom to choose a subject, try freewriting. Most types of business writing, because it is clear from the beginning the material you need to cover, do not lend themselves to this prewriting strategy.

Getting It Right

Effective freewriting is creative. It's about *flow*. To get the most from this technique, you need to allow your mind to wander, making connections that lead from one idea to the next. Rather than listing ideas, you freewrite in paragraph form. But that doesn't mean you should worry about proper sentence structure, spelling, punctuation, or grammar. Don't reread anything you've written until you've finished freewriting.

If the idea of freewriting seems overwhelming, set a timer for 10 minutes. It might seem short, but you'll be surprised to find how much you can write in this time, and there will be less anxiety about the process if you know there is a scheduled end to it.

REMEMBER THIS!

Good ideas may not appear in the first few minutes of freewriting. Don't judge yourself. Continue writing until the timer goes off.

Example

I need to write a paper about Herman Melville, but I'm not sure where to start. I liked Moby Dick, but why was it dedicated to Nathaniel Hawthorne? Did Melville like his wriitng (I don't see any similarities) or where they friends? I should look this up.

What are the connections between Melvilles' life and his work? I know Typpee and Omoo are considered autobiographical, but what about Moby Dick? Does it confine a writer to use his life as subject matter, or does it free him? I've heard Moby Dick is less autobiographical than the other two novels, so maybe I could compare the three against his life story to draw conclusions about autobiography and his creative process.

Why It's Effective

This writer jumped into freewriting hesitantly ("I'm not sure where to start"), but continued until some good ideas emerged. He moves from a seemingly irrelevant question ("why was it dedicated to Nathaniel Hawthorne?") to a valid essay topic (the link between autobiography and the creative process). Obviously, there is more to do before this student begins to write, but the freewriting process has helped to formulate a workable idea.

Here's another example:

OK, perceived job prospects are important but my initial reaction is they put too much weight on this. Most people I know didn't choose their major because of potential jobs but because they like the field, or if they did choose because of a specific job its because they think they'll like that career, of course if there's a high demand for a particular career that does make it more appealing, but for example I'd never switch from biology to computer technology simply because there's a lot of highpaying jobs waiting for me upon graduation. I think comp tech is so popular because kids like computers, not <u>just</u> because those undergrads want good jobs. Another prob: doubt that it's the most popular major because of the success of recent grads. That's always a boost, because it's evidents of a good program. But is that what recruiting should focus on? Yes, eminent profs and grad success rates are important but recruitment should also focus on solidity of program. And what about the other programs at B? What's not said here is what % of students are comp tech majors and how that fits into the overall mission/departmts/programs at the school. (BTW who are those experts? Memo doesn't say.)

Practice 2

Select a general theme, and freewrite for 5 minutes on your own paper. Note that these themes are intentionally general; you must decide how to approach the one you choose.

(A) The Impact of Art on Everyday Life

(B) Cooking

(C) Favorite TV Shows

(D) Work

Journalists' Questions

What It Is

Another effective technique for exploring a topic is to ask the six questions every good journalist uses: who, what, where, when, why, and how? These questions can help you look at your topic more closely, and discover inventive ways of approaching it. Remember that the better you know your topic, the better you can write about it.

Getting It Right

To get the most out of these questions, break them down into subtopics. Every question won't apply to every topic. Be flexible, allowing the nuances of your subject to emerge. The following lists are not exhaustive, but are meant to get you started.

Who:	physical attributes, personality traits, family history, education, occupation
What:	meaning, cause, effect, duration, purpose, limits, parts, history, size
Where:	location, setting description, history, boundaries
When:	time period, frequency, history of occurrence, duration
Why:	causes, motives, results, objectives, reasoning
How:	method, process, procedure, equipment needed, people needed, level of difficulty

> **SHARP WRITING TIP**
>
> Use the journalists' questions (who, what, where, when, why, how) to gather ideas.

Example

You've been assigned to write an essay on Stephen Crane's *The Red Badge of Courage*. A more specific topic has not been determined.

Who: Henry Fleming (protagonist, Union Army soldier in Civil War), Jim Conklin (Henry's friend), Wilson (another friend), tattered soldier, lieutenant, Henry's mother

What: Henry joins army to fight in civil war; questions his courage and manhood; runs away from battle; rejoins regiment and fights courageously; becomes color bearer; feels he has acquired courage and manhood

Where: unspecified, but presumed to be near Chancellorsville, Virginia; open fields, woods, rivers

When: during the civil war (the battle of Chancellorsville took place in early May, 1863)

Why: Henry joins the army because he wants to experience the glory of battle; he realizes that he might be a coward; after running from one battle, he enters the fighting and becomes a fierce soldier; believes he has passed through the "red sickness" of battle; comes to understand what courage and manhood really are

How: Henry grows and changes not only because of battle, but because of encounters with death (corpse in woods, Jim Conklin); he works through his feelings about manhood, courage, and even the meaning of human existence

Why It's Effective

Some of the questions (*where* and *when*) yield simple responses that aren't helpful. But consider the answers to *why*, *what*, and *how*. They repeat a theme that could result in a great essay: the transformation of Henry Fleming from frightened enlistee to valiant soldier. In this case, the exercise is effective because it ellicits a workable idea three times, with slight variations. Have you heard the theory that a writer sometimes doesn't know what she is thinking until she begins to write? In this case, she was probably unaware that she had recognized this theme until after answering all six questions.

Note that many of the journalists' questions could have been answered in various ways. For example, *why* could mean why did Crane write the short novel, why did the story end as it did, why did the protagonist act a certain way, or even why the civil war was fought. All are valid responses. When using this prewriting strategy, allow yourself to answer the questions in whatever way makes sense to you. Some answers may seem offbeat, but they could result in a workable idea.

Practice 3

Read a story in the newspaper, asking the journalists' questions about it. Note the information the printed story didn't cover, but that you'd like to know. What angle did the story take, and what did it ignore?

Journaling

What It Is

Journaling is the process of keeping a written record of your thoughts, experiences, and/or ideas. Depending upon the type of writing you are preparing for, you could try out different topics, write about experiences and anecdotes, or explore some of your likes and dislikes.

Journaling is also a great way to discover your writing voice.

> **FLASHBACK**
>
> As we noted in chapter 4, without voice, writing is dull and lifeless.

As you write to yourself, notice the words you use. What is your tone like? It might be too casual for every occasion, but by keeping and reading your journal, you will begin to hear yourself, and become familiar with your unique voice.

Unlike the other prewriting techniques in this chapter, journaling takes some time. A three-entry journal probably won't offer much insight. But if you have trouble writing, whether for school, business, or personal purposes, or have a long-term writing project assigned, this technique could help you.

If you know you have three months to complete a report, a journal could help you keep track of thoughts and ideas before you begin writing. College application essays that may be written on any topic could also benefit from journaling.

Getting It Right

Three suggestions for keeping a journal are the common blank book, a word processing format, or the increasingly popular online blog (short for *Web log*).

The blank book is portable. If you envision yourself writing in a coffee shop, before class starts, in bed when you wake up, or at the dinner table, this method would work best.

Computer-based journals are great if you don't mind spending more time at the computer and if you write better at a keyboard. Open a new document in your word processing program and begin typing.

If the allure of a potential audience is exciting and motivating, blogging might be the best journaling method for you. The public nature of blogs makes some writers stick with journaling better than if they used another method. If you decide to try blogging, check out a Website such as www.blogger.com, or enter the term *blogging* on a search engine to find hundreds of sites on which you can post your own Web log.

When you've chosen a method, stick with it. Journaling only works if you do it regularly, and stay loosely on topic, whether that means writing about yourself, or thinking of solutions to your company's manufacturing line problems. If you find yourself veering off on wild tangents, follow them for a few paragraphs (you never know when a good idea might emerge).

But if you've got pages of unusable material, it's time to refocus on your topic.

Practice 4

Choose a journal format and describe an incident that happened to you yesterday—not as a journalist would, but as if you were telling a friend about it. Include the setting; the other people involved, if applicable; and the action or actions taken. What made you act/think/feel as you did? Are there any consequences of this incident? Use as many details as you can.

> **REMEMBER THIS!**
>
> **Ruminating** is the process of keeping a subject in mind. Writers who use this technique think frequently, and in many ways, about their topic.

Some writers benefit from ruminating during the prewriting stage. These people will often tell you their best ideas come while driving, shaving, or even dreaming. Allow yourself the freedom to think as if you were free-writing. Let ideas flow from one to another without inhibition. Ruminating doesn't work for everyone, but you won't know if this is a useful technique without trying it.

Reading and Research

What It Is

This prewriting technique uses other sources of information to help you formulate ideas. It's not about plagiarizing, but rather involves diving into your topic to find relevant data, statistics, and other types of information that you can incorporate and agree or disagree with in your writing.

Getting It Right

To use reading and research effectively, you need to know at least generally what your subject is. Look it up at a library or online using a search engine or a general reference site such as:

- www.bartleby.com (searchable encyclopedias, works of literature, dictionaries, and many other full texts)

- www.highbeam.com (free trial membership allows searches of magazines, newspapers, and journals)
- www.loc.gov (Library of Congress site has full texts of historical print materials, international periodicals, many other research tools).

Remember as you read and research that you are prewriting. Don't stray too far from your topic, but be willing to go off on a tangent. For example, if your subject is the use of steroids by athletes, you can find magazine and newspaper articles on specific athletes, legal documents about the consequences of distributing the drugs, medical explanations of the effects steroids have on the body, and colleges' drug use policies.

Reading and research take time. Set aside a few hours to look for, read, and take notes on various sources pertaining to your subject.

Practice 5

On your own paper, using the subject of heirloom vegetables, use a search engine to find information on the Internet. Make a list of five specific sources with pertinent information, with a brief explanation of the type (retail supplier, opinion, news story, how-to, etc.). Next, go to an online library or other research center, and perform another search. Find five more specific sources, and add them to your list. Finally, using those sources, come up with three different topics you could write about on the subject of heirloom vegetables.

STAGE 2: PLANNING

Once you've done some kind of prewriting, you will need to shape the information and ideas you've gathered. Planning means getting ready to write by discovering a main topic, subtopics, and examples or other illustrative forms within your prewriting notes. The following pages explain the most effective ways to transform your notes into a workable, organized writing scheme.

Use a Graphic Organizer

What It Is

A graphic organizer is a visual tool that presents ideas in a connected, clear way. There are many types of graphic organizers, but no matter which one you choose, you will first have to identify your subject, main idea(s), secondary ideas, and examples or details from the prewriting you did in Stage 1. Notice that this list moves from general (subject) to specific (examples and details).

Read through your prewriting and note each category. What stands out as a main idea? Are there related secondary ideas? Do you have details or examples to support your ideas?

Two of the most common graphic organizers are **webs** and **outlines**.

Think of a spider creating a web; she begins in the center, and works her way outward. A writing web is similar. The subject is placed in the center, and spokes radiate out from it. Those spokes are filled in with main ideas (closest to the center), secondary ideas (next closest to the center), and examples or details (furthest from the center).

Most writers are familiar with outlines, even if they've never used one for prewriting. Standard outline form uses Roman and Arabic numerals and upper and lower case letters to arrange ideas, details, and examples. Depending on your subject, you may not use all of these layers; however, main ideas should be placed at capital Roman numerals. Secondary ideas are found at upper case letters and sometimes also Arabic numerals. The details and examples used to support your ideas should be placed at Arabic numerals or lower case letters, depending on how complex your subject is. (The more complex, the more likely you'll have layers of secondary ideas; see the example on the following page.)

I.

    A.

    B.

        1.

        2.

            a.

            b.

                i.

                ii.

You won't use all of these subcategories for every topic. Here's an example:

 I. Intro: College education is a right, not just a privilege. It should be available to every citizen, and those with talent should be offered extra opportunities.

 II. Why it's a right: democracy not meritocracy

   A. Country founded on democratic principle, all created equal, equal opportunity
    1. Principle used throughout primary and secondary schooling
    2. Used in work force, government, law enforcement
    3. Why not higher ed?
    4. Counterargument: high school should be enough to satisfy equality for all principle

 III. Rebuttal: lack of college education limits a whole segment of population, keeps them at lower wages, lower socio-economic status (transition to next para)

 IV. Why meritocracy is a problem

   A. Few in control of many (who decides who can go to college?)
   B. How do you define "talented"?
   C. Ripe for corruption

 V. Benefits of equal opportunity

    1. Less ignorance (thus more tolerance, better health care, less drugs/violence, etc.)
    2. More skilled workforce
    3. Less poverty
    4. More involvement in community and politics

 VI. Conclusion (restate thesis)

Getting It Right

The most important step in graphic organizing is extracting information from your prewriting. You'll probably need to read it a few times to determine how best to organize it. At this stage, you can gather any necessary facts and cut anything that doesn't work. Webs and outlines are flexible, and should be completed in pencil. Rearrange, add, and delete until you are pleased with the result.

If you are making an outline, you'll need to think about how your main ideas relate to one another. Could they be presented in any order, or do they lead from one to another? Do they vary in importance? Arrange them in a way that makes sense. As you create your outline, you may also wish to reword or rephrase your ideas.

Web Example

Let's go back to the brainstorming example earlier in the chapter, and create a web from that list. The writer has checked the OSHA website and determined that mandatory breaks and screening for existing medical conditions are required by law.

improve training for workers	*main idea*
check OSHA website for compliance issues	*main idea*

improve company's safety record—
    list past problems
	main idea
	  with examples

cold weather injuries: detail each one	*secondary idea* *with examples*
how to better treat injuries (train staff)	*secondary idea*
teach warning signs for hypothermia	*example*
mandatory breaks in heated trailer	*secondary idea*
issue of clothing—should we provide?	*secondary idea*
Workers w/existing medical conditions— screening for	*secondary idea*
Provide warm beverages at all work sites	*secondary idea*

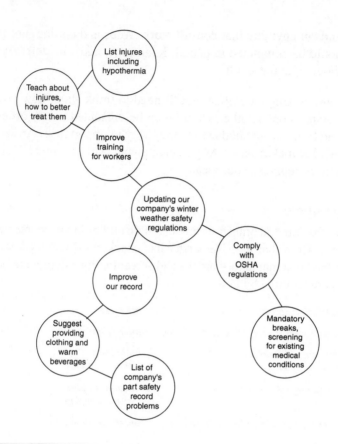

Organize prewriting notes to create a useful plan for writing.

Why It's Effective

The writer has identified three main ideas, which could be used for three body paragraphs in the assigned report. The web shows how they relate to both the subjects and to supporting examples and details. Note that additional information (regarding OSHA regulations) was gathered to answer questions raised in the prewriting stage.

Webs can get as complicated as needed, as you can see on the following page.

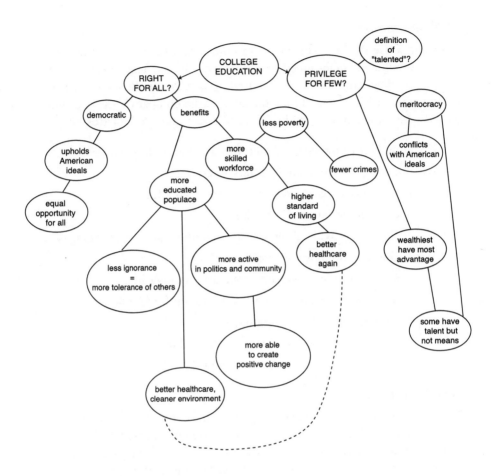

FLASH FORWARD

Chapter 6 will cover how to write the three parts of almost any kind of communication: Introduction, Body, and Conclusion. The subject will be part of your introduction, and main ideas will anchor the body, supported by details and examples.

Outline Example

Let's again use the brainstorming example. The writer has checked the OSHA website and determined that mandatory breaks and screening for existing medical conditions are required by law. He or she also checked company records and found that, throughout the company's history, two workers were treated for hypothermia, and one was treated for frostbite.

I. Updating Our Company's Winter Weather Safety Regulations
   A. Improve Our Company's Safety Record
      1. Past problems and how they were dealt with
         a. hypothermia and frostbite
      2. Suggest providing appropriate clothing and warm beverages
      3. Improve training for workers
         a. hold seminar to teach about cold weather injuries
         b. use signs posted in work areas to reinforce training
      4. Comply with OSHA Regulations
         a. provide mandatory breaks in heated trailers
         b. screen all workers for existing medical conditions

Why It's Effective

This writer found one main idea—improving the company's safety record. He or she determined that looking at past problems, providing clothing and warm beverages, improving training, and complying with Federal regulations were all secondary ideas. Note that the outline form is flexible enough to coordinate these ideas, along with details and examples to support them.

Practice 6

Using the notes you took in practice 3, determine your main idea, secondary idea(s), and details and examples. On the following lines, create a web or outline, adding or deleting information as necessary.

SUMMARY

Prewriting is the first step in the writing process. Its two stages are: (1) gathering ideas and (2) making a writing plan. In this chapter, you learned seven great strategies for successful prewriting:

Brainstorming helps you get ideas from your brain onto the page. It's an active, energetic prewriting strategy in which you list any and every idea you have about a given subject. Don't worry about spelling, grammar, or even making sense when you're brainstorming.

Freewriting is similar to brainstorming, but it works best in paragraph form. When you freewrite, you allow ideas to flow without interruption, editing, or rereading. If you aren't sure where to start your writing, or how to approach a general topic, try freewriting.

Journalists' Questions (who, what, where, when, why, and how) are another great way to explore a writing topic. Remember to get detailed in your answers; *who* isn't just a name, but might also be a physical description, family history, educational background, and/or political leaning. *Why* might include causes, motives, results, objectives, and reasoning.

Journaling is the process of keeping a written record of your thoughts, experiences, and/or ideas. You can use a blank book, word processor, or even an online blog for your journal. Whichever method you choose, it's a great way to discover your writing voice. But, unlike the other prewriting techniques in this chapter, journaling takes some time.

Reading and Research for prewriting uses other sources of information to help you formulate ideas. Libraries, Internet search engines, and online research centers are all good places for reading and research.

Once you have your ideas on paper, you need to organize them before beginning to write. The planning stage of prewriting is when you take a hard look at your notes, and determine what are main ideas, secondary ideas, examples, and details. Then, map them out with a graphic organizer such as a web or outline. Graphic organizers get you ready to write by imposing a framework on your ideas.

PRACTICE EXPLANATIONS AND EXAMPLES

Practice 1

Your brainstorming page should have the topic printed at the top. Your ideas could be words or phrases that are listed, "webbed," or scribbled around the page. They should also be legible.

For example:

Where I Would Like to Live

Beach/ocean

Change of seasons?

Not far from relatives (no California)

Good gardening weather

Culture

Good restaurants

Low taxes

Affordable housing

Practice 2

Your freewriting should be in paragraph form, allowing ideas to flow from one to another. There will probably be spelling and other mechanics errors. Good ideas and direction may not appear until the middle or end of your freewriting.

For example:

Cooking

Why I like to cook. It relaxes me after work. It's fun to share meals with my friends. It feels almost like traveling to another country and experiencing another culture when I dive into an ethnic cookbook. Spicy food is great. I love the smell of exotic spices, and experimenting with flavors. There is always something new to learn. Some of the complicated French recipes are intimidating.

Practice 3

The journalists' questions (*who, what, where, when, why,* and *how*) should be listed, with responses to each. Some responses should involve specula-

PRACTICE EXPLANATIONS AND EXAMPLES *(cont'd)*

tion on what was left out of the news story you read (perhaps the *who* or *when* wasn't specified, or wasn't as detailed as you would have liked).

For example:

Who: elephant in Singapore

What: acupuncture being performed on elephant's leg; it has improved mobility and muscle strength

Where: the Singapore zoo

When: treatment began a month ago, and there are four more months left (does length of treatment depend on progress, or is it predetermined?)

Why: her leg was broken nine years ago by another elephant. She now weighs over 5000 pounds, and was having problems using her leg because of her weight

How: a veterinarian and acupuncturist works on the elephant with handlers who help the elephant cooperate with the treatment (how does treatment differ from that done on humans?)

Practice 4

Your mock journal entry should have a casual tone that you would use to talk with a friend. Did you use details to bring the incident to life? As you reread it, is there an aspect of the incident you hadn't given much thought to, but which now seems important?

For example:

Yesterday my boss called a meeting for the three of us working on the Ogden account. At first I thought something had to be wrong. Which one of us messed up? What happened? When I got into her office, she asked me to sit down with Ken and Mani, who were already there. They both looked nervous. I saw through the blinds that the Ogden group was sitting in the reception area. They were halfway across the building, but I could tell they were chatting and laughing. Why were they here? Our meeting was supposed to be tomorrow. When I sat down I saw my boss smiling. My heart beat faster. She said, "congratulations."

PRACTICE EXPLANATIONS AND EXAMPLES *(cont'd)*

Practice 5

The sources and types of information on your list should be varied. Possible heirloom vegetable topics include: superiority of, history of, health risks of genetically modified organisms (GMOs), propagating techniques, and reasons for maintaining biodiversity.

For example:

Search engine:

1. www.extension.edu University website, definition, why grow, how to save seeds
2. www.bookstore.com Retail site with guides and how-to books
3. www.vegetablecooking.net Recipes, other food information; explains why heirloom varieties taste better, shows how to use them
4. www.seedsoftheearth.com Retail site offering seeds
5. www.oldendays.net Nostalgia site with page on connecting with the past through food; mentions heirloom vegetables as way to step back in time

Online library:

1. American Folklife Center, Library of Congress, Local Legacies project: Maine lumberjacks prepare heirloom varieties of beans with special technique used by Native Americans
2. American Folklife Center, Library of Congress, Local Legacies project: Denver Farmers' Market gives small growers of heirloom vegetables retail exposure
3. American Folklife Center, Library of Congress, Local Legacies project: history of county fairs- judging of heirloom vegetables
4. Science Reference Guides, Library of Congress: list of Internet resources on container vegetable gardens
5. Immigration collection, Library of Congress: laws passed to prevent Chinese immigrants from growing and selling certain vegetables

   Possible topics:

   Heirloom vegetables from Native Americans

   Methods of seed saving

   Laws dealing with heirloom vegetables

PRACTICE EXPLANATIONS AND EXAMPLES *(cont'd)*

Practice 6

If you made a web, it should have the subject at the center, with main ideas surrounding it. Secondary ideas, details, and examples should also be properly placed. You may have had to add or delete information to create a cohesive plan.

If you made an outline, it should show the relationship between main ideas and secondary ideas, and list supporting examples and details.

For example:

I. Acupuncture
    A. History of
    B. Veterinary Use
        1. Case of elephant in Singapore Zoo
           a. description of ailment
           b. treatment
           c. results

CHAPTER 7

Writing

In this chapter, you will learn how to create a rough draft. Although this step in the process is considered the most intimidating, it doesn't have to be.

Think of writing as freewriting with a plan. Let your writing flow unencumbered by worries about revising, editing, or proofreading (those will come later). If your plan is good, your rough draft should be too. All you are trying to achieve in this step is the creation of material that you can later shape into a final piece of writing (except if you are writing a timed essay).

> **FLASH FORWARD**
>
> Timed essays will be covered in chapter 10, Academic Writing.

Let's first look at some general guidelines that will help you create your rough draft. Then, we'll examine the three parts of almost every written communication: the Introduction, Body, and Conclusion.

GENERAL RULES FOR WRITING

Whether you are writing a memo, an academic paper, an essay, or a letter, there are guidelines that can help you. Although the written products are different, all of these formats share a common process that can be made easier when you understand and follow it.

Let It Flow

The first rule is the simplest: write! Put pen to paper or fingers to keyboard and begin. As with freewriting, forget about mechanics and style when you're writing. Let it flow. Using your plan from chapter 5 as your guide, create sentences and paragraphs that communicate your ideas.

Don't worry about including too much information, or writing beyond a specified length. You are creating the raw material from which, with the help of chapter 7, you will create a polished piece of writing.

Write a Thesis Statement

A thesis statement distills the purpose of your writing into one or two sentences. Most writers include it within their introductory paragraph to announce to their readers what is to come. They also typically reword it and insert it in the conclusion. But even if you don't include it directly in your writing, the act of producing a thesis statement will help you to focus as you create your rough draft. Everything you say should relate to the thesis statement—supporting it, explaining it, or giving examples or details of it. If your writing veers away from the thesis statement, you're either off topic or your statement needs revising.

Use Paragraphs

Paragraphs visually display the organization of your writing. When you move on to a new idea, or from one outline heading to another, begin a new paragraph. That's not to say you should worry too much about structure, especially if it gets in the way of your main goal (getting your ideas into a rough draft). But if you separate information logically into paragraphs, it will help you to see where you have sufficient support and where you don't, it will make the process of revising easier, and it will help your reader follow your argument, too.

Make Copies

A little paranoia can help you keep your writing safe. It's unlikely that someone will walk off with the notebook you're writing in, but it's still not a bad idea to make a copy of your prewriting plan and your rough draft. If you're working on a computer, back up your work often. You don't want to have to go back to Square One unless it's to improve your writing.

Go Back to Square One if Necessary

Just because you have a plan doesn't mean you have to slavishly adhere to it; if something isn't working, go ahead and change it. You might need to do some additional research to come up with more or better examples. One of your secondary ideas might seem weak, and need to be either dropped or amended. Remember that your plan is flexible. Add, subtract, or rearrange as necessary.

On occasion, you will find that your entire plan doesn't work. That's when you need to take another look to determine whether any of it is worth saving. Chances are you already have some good ideas. Perhaps one of your secondary ideas should be the main idea, or perhaps a detail could be expanded to create a new focus. Don't abandon your work without trying first to rework it.

> **SHARP WRITING TIP**
>
> Note any general rules you weren't familiar with or have trouble with.

THE INTRODUCTION

What It Is

Good introductions do two things; they announce your subject and they grab (or hook) the reader's attention. Depending on the type of writing you're working on, you might need to write more "announcement" and less "hook."

For example, a business memo should be more straightforward than a college admissions essay. The audience for the memo probably needs to read the information it contains, and would benefit from a direct approach that explains the context and, at least generally, the content, of the memo. But the admissions essay is different. It will be read in 2–3 minutes by an admissions officer who has a stack of essays left to read. He or she doesn't even have to finish your essay. If you tell them what you're going to say in the first paragraph, they'll probably put it down. The admissions essay, therefore, needs more "hook" than "announcement."

Getting It Right: The Thesis Statement

An integral part of most effective introductions (except those acting purely as hooks) is the thesis statement. The statement clearly explains the purpose of your writing in one or two sentences. It serves as a guide to the reader, either as a roadmap ("here's what I'm going to show you") or as a justification for your argument ("this is why this subject is important"). Strong thesis statements take a stand, are specific, and express just one main idea.

Examples

Let's look at a sample thesis statement:

The SUV has been blamed for many of our country's woes.

This is a weak thesis statement for a number of reasons. First, it doesn't take a stand. How does the writer feel about the SUV? We don't know. Second, it's not specific. "Many woes" doesn't tell us whether the argument will be about safety, the environment, gas consumption, or something else entirely.

> **FLASHBACK**
>
> As you saw in chapter 1, the passive voice is often inappropriate in writing. A strong thesis statement that takes a stand should be written in the active voice.

Here's a better example:

SUVs are a threat to the environment. Scientists are warning that their contributions to global warming and air pollution are far greater than most people realize.

Why It Works

This statement works because it takes a stand in the first sentence, and gets specific about it in the second. It has one main idea (SUV as threat to the environment) and is written in the active voice.

> **SHARP WRITING TIP**
>
> Thesis statements should be in the active voice, take a stand, and be specific.

Practice 1

Using your brainstorming notes or freewriting from the first or second practice in chapter 5, come up with a strong thesis statement.

Getting It Right: The Hook

The "hook" part of the introduction can take various forms. Depending on the type of writing you're doing, you might want to startle your reader with some interesting information, illustrate the point you're about to make with a story, or provide some historical background. Hooks can precede or follow the thesis statement. Here are a few ideas for effective hooks:

1. Scene or Anecdote

A scene that illustrates or introduces your thesis statement is a great hook. Anecdotes with details that appeal to the emotions and senses draw the reader in. For example, if you are writing about how expensive it is to live in New York, you could begin with a scene of a middle-class family moving out of the city, leaving their beloved home and friends behind. Their rent-controlled apartment became a condominium and they couldn't afford to buy it. After a long search, they could not find affordable housing.

2. Statistic

Operating under the assumption that numbers don't lie, a statistic can startle the reader, making the information you are about to present more real. Instead of beginning with a thesis statement, "New York is the most expensive U.S. city to live in," consider opening with a statistic. "To get by in New York, you'll need an income of at least $80,000" gets more attention.

3. Quote

Using someone else's words can also grab the attention of your reader. But keep this in mind: a quote works because of the credibility and familiarity of the person quoted, as well as the relevance of the words they used. Therefore, the person (or organization) you're quoting should be familiar to your reader, and that person should say something insightful.

4. Context

If your topic needs some background information to make it more understandable, an opening hook that gives context could work well. Historical, literary, biographical, or scientific background can help the reader understand the problem or question your writing addresses. But consider your audience carefully; what will fascinate some could put others to sleep if they already know it. If you're worried that a few readers might need context, consider including it later in your writing, or as an appendix or footnote.

5. Question

Provocative or puzzling questions immediately draw your reader in because you are simultaneously addressing them directly and asking them to think about your subject. If you use this type of hook, be certain your thesis statement or writing as a whole satisfactorily answers the question!

Practice 2

Building on Practice 1, use your thesis statement and brainstorming notes or freewriting to write two introductory hooks. Choose any of the five types that appeal to you and work well with your topic.

Checklist: Avoid These Mistakes

- **Too Broad:** Sweeping generalizations about the importance or relevance of your topic are boring, and won't relate to your strong thesis statement (which is specific). In addition, such generalizations usually oversimplify. If you're writing about New York as the most expensive place to live, you're writing in the present tense. Your reader won't care if you tell them, "Throughout the history of the United States, New York has been a city where only the wealthiest could live comfortably." They might question your information, too.

- **Repetitious:** If your writing is an assigned topic, don't repeat or reword it. A college admissions essay on the person who has most influenced your life shouldn't begin, "The person who has most influenced my life is…" If your boss asks you to write a report on the reasons why you think the company's client base should be expanded, don't open with, "There are many reasons why I think our company's client base should be expanded." Address the topic immediately, without restating it.

- **Clichéd:** Overused (and therefore boring) openers, cliches are typically questions ("Did you ever wonder…") or context. Resist the urge to repeat what has been written countless times before. One introductory cliché that should never find its way into your writing is the dictionary definition: It's boring and probably too general to shed light on your topic.

THE BODY

What It Is

In the body of your writing, you develop your argument, present your ideas, and analyze your topic. The body is made up of paragraphs that separate ideas and include details, examples, and evidence to support those ideas.

Getting It Right

It's important to let the writing of your rough draft flow. Use your plan as a guide, and remember to use paragraphs to separate ideas. Those paragraphs can be from four to about ten sentences in length, depending upon how much supporting material you include for the main idea of that paragraph. Variety in paragraph and sentence length adds interest. But don't worry too much about structure; your objective is to get a workable draft onto the page.

Most writers are familiar with the rule that one must not use the work of another writer without proper citation. Quotation marks, footnotes, and acknowledgement within the text are all acceptable citations. But what type should be used where? If you aren't sure, you can end up plagiarizing without any intention of doing so. Here are a few simple rules to avoid plagiarism in your writing:

You need a citation when you use:

1. someone else's words or ideas

2. ideas or information given to you in a conversation, interview, or email

3. pictures, diagrams, illustrations, or charts created by someone else

You don't need a citation when you use:

1. your own words to describe your experiences, thoughts, observations, or insights

2. information that could be described as common knowledge (facts that appear in many sources and are known by many people)

Paraphrasing, or putting information you got from another source into your own words, is a great way to avoid plagiarizing when you don't want to use a direct quote. However, you should still credit the original source. For example,

> As the historian Edward Gibbon noted in *The Decline and Fall of the Roman Empire*, Charles V and the Roman emperor Diocletian had much in common.

The writer did not come up with the idea that the two rulers had much in common, but he or she also did not want to quote directly from Gibbon's text. A mention of him and his work is sufficient to give credit for the idea.

THE CONCLUSION

What It Is

As you end your writing, you have another chance to show your reader why everything you've said is important. Your conclusion should answer the question, "So what?" Leave a good last impression with your reader with a strong conclusion that avoids clichés. "To conclude," "To summarize," and "In closing" are boring and overused. Leave them out.

Getting It Right

Conclusions are not the place for introducing new information. But you also don't need a paragraph to repeat everything in the body of your writing. What makes an effective conclusion? Many of the techniques that help create strong introductions also work well as endings.

1. Look to the future. What do you anticipate doing or accomplishing? What outcome do you hope for?

> *We can hope that our government will take a harder look at the problems caused by SUVs, and begin to take action to correct them.*
>
> *If we implement this plan, by next quarter we should begin to see results.*

2. Ask a question. The answer should echo your thesis statement.

   How can the environmental impact of SUVs be lessened?

   What can our company do to improve our bottom line?

3. Issue a call to action. Tell your readers what they should do.

   Begin by making better choices the next time you shop for a car.

   Improve customer relations today by calling or emailing your contact for each account.

4. Remind your reader why your topic is important to them.

   If we are to enjoy a clean environment tomorrow, we must take action today.

   When our company succeeds, every employee reaps benefits as well.

5. Refer to the scene or anecdote used in the introduction.

   The family that had to relocate out of the city could have been helped by these reforms.

Practice 3

Building on Practice 2, use your thesis statement and introductory hooks to write two conclusions. Choose any of the five types that appeal to you and work well with your topic.

VARIETY IN SENTENCE STRUCTURE

You'll want to use a combination of simple, compound, complex, and compound-complex sentences. Here are some examples:

Simple (one main clause):

Any entrepreneur seeking a new business location should seriously consider Nashville, Tennessee.

Compound (two or more main clauses):

Entrepreneurs often need to select a new business location, and they should seriously consider Nashville, Tennessee.

Complex (one main clause, one subordinate clause):

If any entrepreneurs are looking for a new business location, they should seriously consider Nashville, Tennessee.

Compound-complex (two or more main clauses, plus at least one subordinate clause):

Entrepreneurs often need to select a new business location, and when they do, they should seriously consider Nashville, Tennessee.

In addition to using a variety of these basic sentence forms, you can enliven your sentences by placing "interrupters," phrases and clauses in various places:

X is unlike Y because of Z.
Because of Z, X is unlike Y.
However, X is unlike Y because of Z.
X, however, is unlike Y because of Z.
However, because of Z, X is unlike Y.

Practice 4

Each sentence is provided in either **simple**, **compound**, **complex**, or **compound-complex** form. **Rewrite each given example in the three other forms.**

Simple: Sometimes the fresh perspective of a non-expert can be valuable in the consideration of a subject.

Compound: The feeling of having fulfilled a personal goal is important, but the tangible rewards of society are at least as important.

Complex: Even though Company B is more expensive, the important question is whether the combined cost of pest-control and savings in product damage are greater with Company B.

Compound-Complex: Different academic communities have different traditions, and while these differences may be significant, it is an oversimplification to say that there can be no meaningful interaction between them.

Length

Write in a variety of sentence lengths to create rhythm for your readers. A short sentence (four to eight words) can effectively emphasize a simple point; a long sentence (30–45 words) might be necessary to present a relatively complicated idea. However, too many short sentences are likely to sound monotonous while too many long sentences may be difficult on your reader.

> **Example:** Entrepreneurs often need to select a new business location, and when they do, they should seriously consider Nashville, Tennessee. This southern city has a great deal to offer.

Sentence Openers

How you *start* your sentences should vary too. If all of your sentences start with the subject, even if the sentence lengths and forms vary, it can sound awfully tedious (*unless* you are purposely using parallel construction).

> **Monotonous:** Nashville was founded in 1779. Tenessee became the sixteenth state of the union in 1796. Nashville became the state's capital in 1812.

> **Exciting:** Founded in 1779, Nashville became the capital of Tennessee in 1812, sixteen years after Tennessee became the sixteenth state of the union.

To add variety, combine sentences as in the example above and start some sentences with introductory clauses and phrases rather than the subject. But keep the basic order for sentence structure for your core clause (subject, verb, indirect object, object).

> **Needs Variety:** Nashville was founded in 1779. It became the state capital in 1812.

> **Has Variety:** Founded in 1779, Nashville became the state capital in 1812.

A VARIED VOCABULARY

Repetition is one of our most effective rhetorical devices. However, excessive repetition should be avoided; One important sentence-level strategy is to use synonyms instead of relying on a few key words throughout your writing.

> **Repetitive Vocabulary:** <u>Business</u> is not an occupation for the faint of heart. Every <u>businessperson</u> should be aware that nearly 50% of <u>businesses</u> fail in their first year, while 75% of <u>businesses</u> go under within three years. Our first order of <u>business</u> in this essay is to consider the question, "What are the causes of <u>business</u> failure?"

> **Synonym-Enriched:** <u>Business</u> is not an occupation for the faint of heart. Every <u>entrepreneur</u> should be aware that nearly 50% of new <u>ventures</u> fail in their first year, while 75% go under within three years. Our first <u>concern</u> in this essay is to consider the question, "What are the causes of <u>commercial</u> failure?"

An effective way to avoid repetition is to make lists of terms pertinent to the various prompt topics.

Practice 5

The following paragraph contains examples of overly repetitive word use. Correct the problems by rewriting the paragraph with appropriate synonyms in place of the repetitive words and phrases.

> Courses that focus on intellectual development are more important than courses that contribute to professional development. Courses focused on professional development assume that these courses will still be relevant to the future job market, while in fact the constant changes in the job market might make such courses obsolete. In contrast, courses that work toward intellectual development are courses that train a person for a variety of job market roles, so that even if the job market changes, the work done in the courses remains relevant. This is not to say that many courses cannot do both: preparing a person for the job market while also preparing her for a variety of different job market possibilities. But, while courses on professional development have their place in the

realm of university courses, they should not be allowed to supersede courses that train the intellect for a changing job market.

TRANSITIONAL PHRASES

Your writing should be stitched together with transitional phrases. From the second paragraph to the conclusion, each topic sentence should begin with a conspicuous signpost marking the trajectory of your argument: *the first problem, first of all, second, furthermore, one additional factor, in conclusion,* etc.

Below, you'll find a list of some of the most useful transitional words and phrases for your essays.

Purpose	Transitions
Show addition	and, also, again, in addition, furthermore, moreover, besides, next, too
Introduce an example	for example, for instance, such as, in particular, in fact, in other example words, that is, specifically, on the one hand/other, to illustrate
Indicate the passage of time	before, after, afterward, next, during, meanwhile, later, eventually, passage of time in the meantime, immediately, suddenly, finally
Indicate rank	first, second, third, etc. (of all); first and foremost; most important; more importantly; above all
Indicate cause	because, since, for this reason
Indicate effect	as a result, consequently, therefore, hence
Indicate comparison	similarly, likewise, like, just as, in the same manner
Indicate contrast	but, however, on the other hand, on the contrary, conversely, in contrast, yet, whereas, instead, rather, while, although, though, despite
Add emphasis	in fact, indeed, certainly, above all
Summarize or conclude	in sum, in summary, in short, in conclusion, to conclude, to sum or conclude up, that is, therefore

SUMMARY

The most important **general guideline** for producing a first draft is also the simplest: **let your writing flow.** Don't stop to worry about mechanics and style, but do use your writing plan as a guide. Before you begin, create a **thesis statement** that distills your topic into a sentence or two. Your statement should take a stand on one idea, be written in the active voice, and be specific. While writing, **use paragraphs to separate main ideas**, and make copies of your work to safeguard it. Finally, tweak your plan if it has problems. Add or delete, change the order of ideas, or make other necessary modifications.

Good **introductions** announce your topic and grab the reader's attention. You can begin with some general information, and lead up to a strong, precise thesis statement, or begin with the statement, and generally show how you will prove, explain, or argue for or against it. Some writing needs very little announcing, but should begin with a strong hook for the reader. Some good strategies for these types of introductions include the use of an anecdote, statistic, or quotation. Information or facts that startle or elicit an emotional response make good hooks.

The **body** of your writing is where you develop your argument using the ideas and supporting facts and examples from your writing plan. It should be structured in paragraphs that help to visually demarcate different ideas. Remember if you are using words, phrases or ideas from another source, you must credit that source. Even if you are paraphrasing, the originator of ideas that aren't your own must be mentioned.

Good **conclusions** avoid two mistakes: they don't repeat everything you've already said, and they don't introduce new information. Strong conclusions leave a great final impression while answering the question, "So what?" End your writing with a strategy similar to one you used in your introduction.

As you write, vary your vocabulary as well as the length and complexity of your sentences, and use transitions that make it easier for a reader to follow your reasoning.

PRACTICE EXPLANATIONS AND EXAMPLES

Practice 1

Your thesis statement should tell, in one or two sentences, what you are going to write about (a roadmap statement) or why your topic is important (a justification statement). It should be written in the active voice, and take a stand. Only one main idea should be expressed, and that idea should be specific.

For example:

Cooking not only helps me relax and entertain my friends, but it allows me to experience other cultures.

Practice 2

If you used a scene or anecdote in your introduction, does it illustrate or introduce your thesis statement? Does it contain details that appeal to the emotions and senses?

If you used a statistic, does it have the power to startle your reader? Do the numbers make your topic seem more real?

If you used a quote, the person you quoted should be familiar to your reader, and the words should be insightful.

If you provided context, does it give background information that helps your reader understand the problem or question your writing addresses? If you asked a question, your thesis statement should answer it.

For example:

How can you experience another culture without leaving your home?

The smell of toasting cardamom and coriander filled the kitchen as I chopped the fresh garlic, ginger, and onions.

Practice 3

Your conclusions should not begin with a cliché such as "In conclusion," or "To summarize." You may have provided a vision of your topic in the future, given your reader a call to action, or reminded him or her why your topic is important. Or, you may have asked a question that can be answered by your thesis statement. If you used a scene or anecdote in your introduction, you could refer to it again in your conclusion.

PRACTICE ANSWERS AND EXAMPLES *(cont'd)*

For example:

My credit card never left my wallet, and I didn't have to wait in lines at the airport, but I felt as if I'd just returned from a night out in Bagalore.

The table was cleared, the pots and pans were washed and put away, and the stove was scrubbed. But my kitchen was still fragrant with curry, chutney, and basmati rice.

Practice 4

Simple	Sometimes the fresh perspective of a nonexpert can be valuable in the consideration of a subject.
Compound	Experts often have the best advice about a subject, but some times the fresh perspective of a non-expert can be valuable too.
Complex	Although experts often have the best advice about a subject, sometimes the fresh perspective of a non-expert can be valuable too.
Compound-Complex	Because experts typically have the most information about a subject, they often have the best advice about that subject, but sometimes the fresh perspective of a non-expert can be valuable too.

Simple	The tangible rewards of society are at least as important as the feeling of having fulfilled a personal goal.
Compound	The feeling of having fulfilled a personal goal is important, but the tangible rewards of society are at least as important.
Complex	Although the feeling of having fulfilled a personal goal is important, the tangible rewards of society are at least as important.
Compound-Complex	Rewards are important, and although the feeling of having fulfilled a personal goal is important, the tangible rewards of society are at least as important.

Simple	The important question is whether the combined cost of pest-control and savings in product damage are greater with Company B.
Compound	The important question is not which pest-control company is cheaper, but rather which company provides the best combination of cost and savings in product damage.
Complex	Even though Company B is more expensive, the important question is whether the combined cost of pest-control and savings in product damage are greater with Company B.
Compound-Complex	Even though Company B is more expensive, if the combined cost of pest-control and savings due to product damage is greater, then Company B is a better deal overall.

Simple	It is an oversimplification to say that there can be no meaningful interaction between academic communities with different traditions.
Compound	Different academic communities have different traditions, but it is an oversimplification to say that these differences preclude meaningful interaction between them.
Complex	Even though different academic communities may have different traditions, it is an oversimplification to say that there can be no meaningful interaction between them.
Compound-Complex	Different academic communities have different traditions, and while these differences may be significant, it is an oversimplification to say that there can be no meaningful interaction between them.

PRACTICE ANSWERS AND EXAMPLES *(cont'd)*

Practice 5

Answers will vary slightly.

Repetitive words and phrases in this paragraph: *courses, development, job market*

Synonyms for "courses": *lessons, classes, curricula, programs, learning, education*

Synonyms for "development": *improvement, training, education, advancement, enhancement*

Synonyms for "job market": *employment, professional setting, occupation, trade, the world of work*

Sample rewrite using these synonyms:

A curriculum that focuses on intellectual improvement is more important than a curriculum that contributes to professional training. An educational program that emphasizes professional advancement assumes that this education will still be relevant to the future occupation of the student, while in fact the constant changes in the job market might make such learning obsolete. In contrast, a course of study that works toward intellectual growth trains a person for a variety of occupational roles, so that even if the demands of employers change, the educational program remains relevant. This is not to say that many curricula cannot do both: preparing a person for employment in a specific field while also preparing her for a variety of potential vocations. But, while classes that provide professional training have their place in the realm of university curricula, they should not be allowed to supersede education that trains the intellect for the ever-changing world of work.

CHAPTER 8

Revising, Editing, and Proofreading

In this chapter, you'll learn how to hone your rough draft at two levels.

First, you will consider broad issues. How well do you address your topic? Does your writing flow? Are your ideas well supported?

Second, you'll examine the draft more closely, looking at sentences, word choices, and mechanics. Is there variety in sentence length and structure? Are the words you've chosen fresh and appropriate for your audience? Are there errors in punctuation, grammar, and spelling? Knowing how to edit your own work is a critical skill that will significantly improve your writing.

PROFESSIONAL EDITING STRATEGIES

Those who make their living as editors have some tricks and tips that all writers can use to make the process of refining a rough draft easier and more thorough.

Wait

The longer you take between the time you finish writing and the time you begin fine-tuning, the greater the chance you'll see it with fresh eyes. A minimum of twenty minutes is recommended; some editors wait at least 24 hours before taking another look.

Speak

Reading your writing aloud may help you to catch awkward passages, word choices, and other errors that looked fine on paper.

Slow down

Reading at a normal pace is too fast to catch errors.

Print

Many editors find it is easier to revise, edit, and proofread on paper than on a computer screen. Print out a copy and mark it up as you find areas for improvement. You may want to make changes after revising and print out a new copy for editing, repeating the process before proofreading.

Back up

A great tip for proofreading is to read backwards, one word at a time. You have a better chance of finding misspelled words (especially those not caught by a spell check program), missing words, and misused words.

Learn from past mistakes

Keep your Sharp Writing guide with you as you edit. Look for the mistakes you make frequently.

Enlist help

Ask a friend or colleague whose skills you trust to read your writing. They may catch errors you missed and be able to point out areas that don't make sense, or need additional explanation.

> **SHARP WRITING TIP**
>
> Make note of any or all of the editors' tips.

REVISING

What It Is

"Re-vision" means literally to see again. When applied to writing, it means looking at your rough draft with "fresh eyes," as if you're the reader and not the writer. This kind of objectivity is needed to find and fix errors.

Some writers avoid the revision process because, once their writing is on paper or computer screen, it seems "good enough." They're willing to proofread, correcting the obvious errors, but stop short of revision, which considers the quality of their work more generally. Most great writers, however, confide that revision is everything; their work would not be nearly as good if they weren't better at "re-visioning" than they were at writing a first draft. Don't think of revising as an optional step; it's part of the writing process.

> **REMEMBER THIS!**
>
> Editing is about fixing what isn't working. Don't rewrite your entire piece of writing; enjoy those paragraphs, sentences, and word choices that work well. Focus on those areas that could be stronger or better organized to convey your intended meaning. Correct grammar, spelling, or punctuation errors.

Successful revision involves two areas of concern: clarity and organization. Take your time as you answer the following questions, looking at your writing repeatedly to find areas for improvement.

Questions for the Revision Process

Clarity:

Does your thesis statement accurately describe the goal of your writing?

Does your writing maintain focus on the topic?

Is each main idea closely related to your topic?

If you're making an argument or explaining a process, are all relevant steps included?

Does the introduction clearly announce your topic and engage your reader's interest?

Is there a clear sense of purpose throughout your writing?

Does your tone support the nature of your writing (formal, casual, business, etc.)?

Structure:

Do your main ideas follow a logical order?

Is each idea supported by examples, details, and/or evidence?

Compare your writing to your prewriting plan; if it doesn't follow it exactly, is there a good reason why you rearranged it?

Is each idea developed sufficiently?

Is sentence structure varied?

Is there unnecessary repetition of ideas?

Getting It Right

There are a number of effective ways to remedy clarity problems. They include:

1. Refining your thesis statement if it's too broad

2. Adding text that provides relevant information that was missing from your first draft

3. Rewriting your introduction to clarify your topic

When you feel you've successfully addressed any clarity issues, go over your writing once again, asking the same questions. Don't stop the process until you're satisfied with your results.

If you find problems with structure, try one or more of the following:

1. Change the order of your paragraphs if your main ideas would make more sense arranged differently. You may need to rework the topic sentences of those paragraphs, or add transitional sentences, to make the new order flow.

2. Add more or better evidence, details, and examples if an idea needs further support, especially if all other main ideas are better supported.

3. If an idea needs development, consider that you may intuitively know that idea, but while writing it may have left out a step. It may be easier to explain it aloud first, and then write it down.

4. Eliminate ideas and phrases that are repetitious or otherwise unnecessary.

5. If there is little sentence structure variation, try combining a few shorter sentences, dividing longer ones, and adding or deleting introductory phrases (if there are too few or too many).

Examples

1. The War of 1812, sometimes called the "Second War for Independence" marked the end of a near century-long conflict between America and Britain. The first War for Independence (the Revolutionary War) ended with the formation of the United States of America as a separate country that was no longer a British colony. The British lost land, including vital trade routes, after that war. The Native American leader Tecumseh, who was pushing for a separate state for his tribes to be located south and west of Lake Erie, along with so-called War Hawks like Henry Clay of Kentucky, helped push the Americans into a war with Britain.

This paragraph begins with a strong thesis statement, which declares that the War of 1812 "marked the end of" the "conflict between America and Britain." It gives some historical context, explaining why the conflict began. But then it veers off course. The topic is the end of the conflict with Britain, and not who pushed us into the war. The last sentence therefore does not support the topic. Either it needs to be dropped, or the thesis statement needs to be reworded. The writer decided to remove the last sentence, and instead continue to introduce the general argument about the conflict. Here is the revised version:

> The War of 1812, sometimes called the "Second War for Independence" marked the end of a near century-long conflict between America and Britain. The first War for Independence (the Revolutionary War) ended with the formation of the United States of America as a separate country that was no longer a British colony. The British, who ruled Canada, lost land, including vital trade routes, after that war. There was bitterness and distrust between the two neighboring nations as a result.

2. We had a sales meeting on Friday. Everyone on the team was in attendance. It went well. We discussed last year's goals. Many of them were reached. We came up with goals for this year. They are more ambitious than last year's.

This paragraph conveys information about the meeting, but it's dull. Every sentence is eight words or less in length, sounding as if they were written for an audience of beginning readers. To correct it, make some sentences longer, while leaving others short. In addition, change some word choices to make the new sentences flow.

> We had a sales meeting on Friday with everyone on the team in attendance. The meeting went well. We discussed last year's goals,

many of which were reached. We also devised goals for this year, which are more ambitious.

Practice 1

Take one or two paragraphs of your rough draft (or any other writing you'd like to revise), and check for clarity and organization problems. Rewrite and rearrange until you are satisfied with the results.

PROOFREADING

What It Is

Some writers consider proofreading a quick run of their computer's grammar and spell check programs. While those programs do find errors, reliance on them to find every mistake is itself a mistake!

Do your own proofreading, and then carefully use grammar and spell check to search for errors you may have missed (see suggestions for their use in the last section of this chapter).

Working from a hard copy, examine your writing one sentence at a time. Mark problems with a pencil as you find them. You might circle words you want to replace, cross out what could be deleted, and make notes about other possible changes in the margin.

As you examine the mechanics of your writing, check for one type of error at a time. That means for each of the following questions, you will read through your entire piece. This method helps you maintain focus and catch more mistakes than you would trying to keep all of the questions in mind at once.

SHARP WRITING TIP

When proofreading, check for one type of error at a time.

Questions for the Proofreading Process

- Are all words used correctly? Review the confused and misused word lists in chapter 2 for guidance.
- Are there too many or too few commas? Check chapter 3 for tips on correct usage.
- When using quotation marks, did you place all sentence-ending punctuation inside them?
- Is there a good balance of contractions (not too few or too many)?
- Do all subjects and verbs agree? Review the section on subject/verb agreement in chapter 2.
- Has the active voice been used whenever possible? Check chapter 2 for an explanation of the inappropriate uses of the passive voice.
- Are there any sentence fragments or run-on sentences? chapter 2 shows how to find and fix them.
- Are there too many or too few adjectives and adverbs?
- Are there any unnecessary verb tense shifts? Review this subject in chapter 2.
- Are all pronoun references clear? Review the section on pronouns in chapter 1.
- Have all modifiers been used correctly?
- Are all apostrophes used correctly? Pay careful attention to possessives, and check chapter 3 for information on correct usage.
- Do any lists of items contain mistakes in parallel structure? See chapter 2 for a quick review of this topic.
- Have all hyphenated and compound words been used correctly? Review the section on dashes in chapter 3.

Getting It Right

The goal of proofreading is to eliminate poor word choices and errors in mechanics. Remove or replace words and phrases that don't work, and correct mistakes such as unnecessary verb tense shifts and confusing pronoun usage. After proofreading, your writing will be more fresh, original, interesting and understandable.

Example

The problems with my dishwasher began a weak ago. I ran a cycle, and the detergent dispenser didn't open. I tried again and it worked. The next day, I ran it, and, it leaked.

Caused a flood in my kitchen. I hired a plumber to fix the leak, but when I try to run it again, it isn't starting. An appliance repair person told me the motor died, and I would have to spend about $300 to replace it.

This paragraph has numerous errors, none of which were caught by grammar or spell check. They include a misused word (*weak* instead of *week*), a sentence fragment (*caused a flood in my kitchen*), and incorrect comma use (*the next day, I ran it, and, it leaked*). Here's the proofread and corrected version:

> The problems with my dishwasher began a **week** ago. I ran a cycle, and the detergent dispenser didn't open. I tried again and it worked. **The next day, I ran it and it leaked, causing a flood in my kitchen**. I hired a plumber to fix the leak, but when I **tried** to run it again, it **didn't start.** An appliance repair person told me the motor died, and I would have to spend about $300 to replace it.

PROOFREADER'S MARKS

Save yourself time and make your notes clearer by using standard proofreader's marks. Here are the most common ones.

¶	Begin new paragraph
No ¶	No new paragraph
ℓ	Delete (with line through all that is to be deleted)
⌒	Close up; delete space
ℓ	Delete and close up (to delete letters within a word)
#	Insert space between two words or elements (put a vertical line between the words or elements)
eq #	Make space equal (between words or lines)
lc	Lowercase
uc	Uppercase

[	Move left
]	Move right
] [	Center
fl	Flush left
fr	Flush right
//	Align
sp	Check spelling or spell out
stet	Let it stand (with dotted line under the text that is to be left to stand as it was originally)
∿ *trans*	Transpose (with a line curved around the text that is to be transposed)
ital	Set in italic type (with text underlined thta is to be italicized)
rom	Set in roman (plain) type (circle the text to be set in roman type)
bf	Set in boldface type (with wavy line under text to be boldfaced)
caps	Capitalize letter (or three underscores under the letter(s) to be capitalized).
∧	Insert here
∧,	Insert comma
V	Insert apostrophe (or single quotation mark)
V	Insert quotation marks (also used for superscript)
⊙	Insert period

?/   Insert question mark (also used for exclamation point)

⊙   Insert semicolon

⊙   Insert colon

=   Insert hyphen

$\frac{1}{m}$ or $\frac{1}{n}$ Insert dash

(/)   Insert parentheses

Practice 2

Exercise 1

Proofread the following paragraph, making all necessary changes and corrections.

Eliza Lynch was an Irish women living in Paris, when she met Francisco

Lopez, son of the dictator of Pariguay. Traveling with him for three

months back to his native land, she had five sons. Lynch remains in

Pariguay for 15 years. While her adopted country was at war with three

neighboring nations, the overseeing of the building of opera houses and

palaces, acquisition of almost half the land in the country, and amassing

of a fortune in gold and jewels was accomplished by "La Lynch", as the

Paraguayans called her. The population and economy during that time.

Only 10% of Paraguayan males survived the war, and over 1 million citizens lost there lives. Although today she is revered with a majestic shrine in Asuncion, many historians believes she was a powerful affluence on Lopez, and had no concern for the people of Paraguay.

Directions for Exercises 2 and 3: Each of the following paragraphs includes even more errors than you found in Exercise 1. Locate and correct all the errors in each paragraph.

Exercise 2

(1) The advise given to the company managers that hiring more additional workers will result in a larger number of houses being built contain a fallacy of exclusion. (2) Several pieces of extremely vital information are not taken into consideration in the reasoning that more workers means more houses built, a moments reasoning reveals that many factors other then merely the number of workers determines the answer to the question of how many houses will be built? (3) For example, if the construction company doesn't have enough construction equipment/tools to equip more worker's, then extra workers won't help irregardless. (4) If there aren't enough building sights available, a raw materials shortage, or sufficient infrastructure to support additional workers, then hiring more workers might well been just a waste of money. (5) The whole question of diminishing returns is not considered by this line of reasoning at all in increasing staff size.

Exercise 3

(1) While the School Boards argument that eating breakfast is related to a reduction of absenteeism in the school breakfast program may be convincing. (2) The conclusion that forcing more students to eat breakfast on the school program will cause a decreasing drop in absences is unwarranted. (3) The statistic's show a correspondance that is far from clear enough to assume causation. (4) The attendance of students at the school-sponsored breakfast program and at subsequent classes maybe both result from a third, unexamined cause that creates the observed affect. (5) For example, students who eat school breakfasts everyday might just happen to be the ones who go to bed early, and therefore are up in time for both the breakfast and for classes. (6) Or maybe the students with better attendance experience a different kind of parent supervision that contributes to both one's better diet and their improved attendance.

GRAMMAR AND SPELL CHECK SOFTWARE

While both of these word processing features are useful, they aren't foolproof. Grammar and spell check software can miss errors, and flag correct usage as mistakes. A recent university study concluded that students with strong language skills, relying on these programs, made almost as many errors as a group with weaker skills who proofread without grammar and spell check.

It's still not a bad idea to use grammar and spell check. But run them as a skeptic. Don't automatically make every change they suggest, or assume that they're always right. You need to think, and use resources such as dictionaries and the grammar, mechanics, and style chapters in this book.

> **SHARP WRITING TIP**
>
> Use, but don't rely exclusively on, grammar and spell check software.

Grammar Check

Run a grammar check program on your writing after you've finished revising and proofreading. Even if you've set it to check as you type, it's a good idea to run it one more time to find any additional errors.

Grammar Check Settings

To modify the grammar check settings in Microsoft Word®, open a blank document and:

1. Click on "Tools" on the toolbar at the top

2. Select "Spelling and Grammar"

3. Click on "Options"

4. Left-click on the options you want, and check the writing style; for most written communications, "standard" is preferred, but the style can also be set to casual, formal, technical, or custom

5. Select "settings" and left-click to choose how many spaces there should be between sentences, whether punctuation should be placed inside quotation marks, and many other options

6. Click on "OK"

Grammar check won't catch every mistake. Pronoun references and dangling modifiers are examples of possible errors that grammar check won't even look for. Here are a few specific mistakes grammar check missed:

- Sasha are going to the concert after he eat his dinner.

Grammar check flagged the first subject-verb agreement error (*Sasha are*), but not the second (*he eat*).

- The bus for which we waited for was already full.

Grammar check finds no errors in this sentence, which uses the preposition "for" twice.

When grammar check highlights an error, it offers a correction, or choice of corrections. You first need to determine whether the "error" is real. If it is, you then need to decide whether any of the corrections are right. Don't guess. Get help in the form of section I of this book, trusted online grammar and mechanics sites, and reference books on English usage. For example:

- South America a lovely vacation destination, is also a bargain.

Grammar check's suggestion for this sentence is to remove the comma. In fact, the comma is correct, but an additional comma after *America* is needed to set off the phrase "a lovely vacation destination."

- While eating her lunch.

Grammar check catches this sentence fragment and suggests revising it. But what if the writer revises it by adding "the doorbell rang?" Now the sentence fragment is a dangling modifier, and grammar check won't flag it.

Using Spell Check

Run spell check on all of your writing, but don't rely on it to be perfect. When you type a real word that isn't the one you intended (*four* instead of *for*, for example), it probably won't be caught.

Let's sew on the bottoms we got from your old sweater.

This writer typed "bottoms" instead of "buttons," and "from" instead of "for," creating a sentence that makes no sense. However, neither error was caught by spell check.

Spell check will also identify correct words as misspelled. It uses a dictionary of over 100,000 words, but that number represents only about half of the commonly used words in English today. Add most proper nouns and industry-specific terms to the list of missing words for a total of hundreds of thousands of words spell check won't recognize, and possibly consider misspelled.

When you do misspell a word, don't rely on spell check's suggestion for the correction. It may not be right. This happens frequently when your misspelling is inadvertently closer to another real word than to the one you intended. For example, if you leave out the "c" from the word *balcony*, you'll be prompted to change the word to *baloney*. Don't automatically select spell check's first suggested corrections; review them carefully before fixing any of your errors.

Most spell check programs allow you to add words to their dictionary. As you type, include correct but flagged words, such as your name, your company or school's name, other proper nouns, and words pertaining to your line of work or field of study. It will save time and effort in the future.

SHARP WRITING TIP

Take advantage of spell check features, such as the ability to add words to the dictionary.

Practice 3

Type the paragraph from Practice 2, Exercise 1 into a blank word processing document. Check the setting for grammar and spell check, and run the software. Compare the results with the answers found at the end of this chapter. Which errors did those programs find, which did they miss, and which were incorrectly flagged as mistakes?

SUMMARY

Revising means looking at your rough draft objectively, as if you're the reader and not the writer. This critical step in the writing process examines the large issues of clarity and organization in your draft. You might find that you need to refocus your thesis statement if it's too broad, or add text that provides missing but relevant information. Change the order of your paragraphs if your main ideas would make more sense arranged differently, or add more or better evidence, details, and examples. Improvements such as these will assure that you've said what you intended to say and that your readers will understand you.

Proofreading helps to eliminate poor word choices and errors in mechanics. Print out a copy of your writing, and review it one sentence at a time. Use the professional editing strategies at the beginning of this chapter to find words and phrases that don't work and mistakes such as subject/verb agreement and misplaced modifiers. Check for one type of error at a time by asking the Proofreaders' Questions. As you make changes, read your work aloud, and ask a friend or colleague to check it, to determine whether you've remedied the problems. Proofreading removes the "little" mistakes that can make your work seem sloppy and reflect poorly on your skills as a writer.

Grammar and spell check software can find many errors, but they also miss errors, and flag correct usage as mistakes. Use them skeptically, assuming they're not always right. Use resources such as dictionaries and this book to check errors and determine the correct remedy.

PRACTICE ANSWERS AND EXPLANATIONS

Practice 1

Your revision should have checked for problems with clarity and structure by asking each of the questions listed. Did you use the suggested remedies to these problems? After revising, you should have asked the questions again to determine whether your revised version includes any clarity or structure issues.

Practice 2

Exercise 1

Eliza Lynch was an Irish woman [changed from incorrect *women*] living in Paris [comma deleted] when she met Francisco Lopez, son of the dictator of Paraguay [corrected spelling]. She traveled for three months with him back to his native land, and had five sons [reworded dangling modifier—Lynch did not have five sons in that time]. Lynch remained [changed present tense to past—shift was unnecessary] in Paraguay for 15 years. While her adopted country was at war with three neighboring [corrected spelling] nations, "La Lynch," [comma placed within quotation marks] as the Paraguayans called her [changed rest of sentence to active voice] oversaw the building of opera houses and palaces, acquired almost half the land in the country, and amassed a fortune in gold and jewels. The population and economy during that time were ruined [added words to make fragment a complete sentence]. Only 10% of Paraguayan males survived the war, and over 1 million citizens lost their [changed word from incorrect *there*] lives. Although today she is revered with a majestic shrine in Asuncion, many historians believe [changed from *believes* to agree with subject *historians*] she was a powerful influence [changed word from incorrect *affluence*] on Lopez, but had no concern for the people of Paraguay.

Exercise 2

(1) The advice given to the company managers that hiring additional workers will result in a larger number of houses being built contains a fallacy of exclusion. (2) Several pieces of vital information are not taken into consideration in the reasoning that more workers means more houses built, and a moment's thought reveals that many factors other than merely the number of workers determines the answer to the question of how many houses will be built. (3) For example, if the construction company doesn't have enough construction equipment or tools to equip more workers, then extra workers won't help regardless. (4) If there aren't enough building sites available, enough raw materials, or sufficient infrastructure to support additional workers, then hiring more workers might well be just a waste of money. (5) The whole question of diminishing returns in increasing staff size is not considered by this line of reasoning at all.

(1) Advice is the noun; advise is a verb.

More additional is redundant.

Advice is the singular subject of the sentence, so it takes the singular verb form, *contains*.

(2) *Extremely vital* is redundant.

This sentence is a run-on—two independent clauses joined by a comma with no conjunction. Fix it by either adding a conjunction or by making it into two sentences (or possibly by swapping the comma for a semicolon).

Moment's is possessive here, so it takes an apostrophe.

Reasoning is repetitive with the preceding clause, so swap it out for another term such as thought.

The sentence compares the number of workers with the other factors, so the comparative *than* is required.

The final question is embedded, so it takes a period rather than a question mark.

(3) Omit the slash as a substitute for the conjunction *or* in essays.

Workers is a simple plural here, so no apostrophe is necessary.

Always use *regardless* rather than *irregardless*.

PRACTICE ANSWERS AND EXPLANATIONS *(cont'd)*

(4) The sentence here refers to building locations (*sites*), not things seen (*sights*).

The middle term in this series violates parallelism in the original, creating confusion.

The future conditional subjunctive here takes the verb *be* rather than *been*.

(5) The phrase in *increasing staff size* modifies the question of diminishing returns, so put the modifier next to the thing it modifies in order to avoid confusion.

Exercise 3

(1) While the school board's argument that eating breakfast in the school breakfast program is related to a reduction of absenteeism may be convincing, (2) the conclusion that forcing more students to eat breakfast on the school program will cause a decrease in absences is unwarranted. (3) The statistics show a correspondence that is far from clear enough to assume causation. (4) The attendance of students at the school-sponsored breakfast program and at subsequent classes might both result from a third, unexamined cause that creates the observed effect. (5) For example, students who eat school breakfasts every day might just happen to be the ones who go to bed early [no comma] and therefore are up in time for both the breakfast and for classes. (6) Or perhaps the students with better attendance experience a different kind of parent supervision that contributes to both their better diet and their improved attendance.

(1) *School board* is a common noun, so there should be no capitals. If it were the name of a specific school board, for example the Shelby County School Board, then it would be capitalized.

In the school breakfast program modifies *eating breakfast*, so it should go closer to what it modifies in order to avoid confusion about what exactly is in the program.

This sentence is a fragment because of the subordinate *while* at the beginning. One easy way to fix this problem is to join it to the next sentence by changing the period to a comma and eliminating the capital letter at the beginning of the next sentence as shown.

(2) *Decreasing drop* is redundant.

PRACTICE ANSWERS AND EXPLANATIONS *(cont'd)*

(3) *Statistics* is a simple plural, not a possessive, so no apostrophe is needed.

Correspondence is misspelled.

(4) *Maybe* is a lowbrow qualifier; prefer *might* or *perhaps*.

Effect is the noun that describes an influence or outcome. The noun *affect* is psychological jargon for "emotion."

(5) The word *everyday* means "ordinary." The phrase *every day* means "happening on each day."

The phrase that follows the conjunction *and* is not an independent clause (it shares its subject with the clause before the conjunction) so the comma is omitted in this case.

(6) *Maybe* is a lowbrow qualifier; *might* or *perhaps* is preferable.

Keep the perspective consistent, and try to avoid the use of *one* as a pronoun.

Practice 3

Note that the answer for Practice 2, Exercise 1 corrects ten errors; grammar and spell check caught just four. They were the misspellings of *Paraguay* and *neighboring*, the sentence fragment, and the confusion of *their/there*.

Sharper Writing Formats

CHAPTER 9

Business Writing

Formats are the framework of written documents. They act as a blueprint, showing the layout and visual style of a type of writing. When you see a person's name and address centered at the top of a page, and their business and educational experiences listed down the page on the left, you know you're looking at a résumé. When you read "Dear _____," you know you have a letter. These formats are familiar to most people, but mistakes are still frequently made with them in business, personal, and academic settings.

Business writing takes many forms, from the résumé that gets you hired, to informal emails, to highly organized, formal reports. Some are created for internal use, meaning they are sent within a company or institution. Others are meant for an audience outside the company. All of these documents are written in specific formats that act as a roadmap for the writer as well as the reader. The writer uses each standard format as a framework for his or her ideas—one that is instantly recognizable by the reader.

Many word processing programs, including Word®, have formatting templates for most business documents. However, before you use them, read through this chapter and understand exactly what is required of each type of document. Determine the formatting protocol of your company; is there a standard form for memos? a preferred letter format? are proposals styled as memos or reports? Don't deviate from the accepted formats, whether they're those of your company or conventional practice.

> **SHARP WRITING TIP**
>
> Always check to see if writing formats are specified by your employer; don't "get creative" and use an unusual format.

RÉSUMÉS

Résumés are summaries of job applicants' education, experience, and relevant skills. They are written for one specific purpose: to get a potential employer interested in hiring the applicant. When you write or rewrite your résumé, keep that purpose in mind. Your résumé is an advertisement that's designed to sell *you*. It must catch the reader's attention and convince him or her that you are the right person for the job.

Getting It Right: Form

Job competition is fierce. When a position is advertised, employers may receive hundreds of responses. To weed out the weak candidates and find the strong ones, just a minute or two is spent reading each résumé. How can you make yours stand out?

Begin by making it look perfect. It should be on high-quality paper and printed cleanly. Your résumé should be balanced and easy to read, with adequate margins and no crowding. Here are some other tips for creating a great-looking résumé:

- Use the best quality paper you can afford, standard letter-size, in white, ivory, or cream.
- Place your name and contact information at the top of every page.
- Use a 12-point font that is easy to read, such as Times New Roman (your name should be slightly larger and boldface).
- Do not use more than two fonts.
- Use the editing tips in chapter 7 to clean up your résumé; there is no excuse for a spelling, grammar, or punctuation error.
- Use bulleted lists; they highlight main points and are easy to read.
- Avoid distracting graphics such as boxes and lines.
- Maintain consistency in the use of boldface, capitalization, underlining, italics, dates, bullets, and spacing.
- Keep it to one page if possible, but don't crowd it.
- Review chapter 4 on clarity and concision. Don't use four words when two will do.

Getting It Right: Substance

The two most important categories of information on a résumé are your professional experience and education. Put experience first if you have plenty of relevant employment to emphasize. Education should be first if you have recently completed or are about to complete a degree, and have little work experience.

SHARP WRITING TIP

Placement of education and experience on a résumé is based on what you want to emphasize; the stronger of the two should come first.

When listing your **work history**, begin with the most recent job, and work backwards chronologically. Include the name, city or town, and state of each employer (complete contact information is not necessary). Use strong verbs to describe your duties and achievements, and mention any awards, special recognition, and/or promotions you received. **Volunteer work**, **military service**, and **internships** can also constitute professional experience; include them if they're relevant to the position for which you are applying.

Educational experience should also be presented in reverse chronological order. Include the name of the institution, your major, the degree you received or are working toward, and your grade point average if it is 3.0 or above (there's no need to mention anything that isn't a positive). If you won any awards, honors, or commendations, highlight them. If you did not complete a degree, you should still include this section, and mention professional study, training received for a job, home study, or credits earned toward a degree.

If it's not clear from your experience or education the type of position you are seeking, you may want to begin your résumé with an **objective statement**. It should be a concise sentence. Don't be general or vague. "I am seeking a challenging position that will enable me to contribute to the advancement of the company while affording me the opportunity for growth and advancement," tells the reader nothing, and wastes space on your résumé. Only use an objective statement if you can write one that is clear and specific.

Involvement in **professional** and **community organizations** should also be included on your résumé if they have some connection with the position for which you're applying. **Leadership roles** should be highlighted, but think twice about mentioning your affiliation with any group that might offend a potential employer.

Personal information such as nationality, race, religion, and gender do not belong on your résumé. Many résumé experts counsel that even hobbies and interests should be left out. Those that recommend them advise their inclusion if they relate to the position, or if they will otherwise help "sell" you. Remember, don't include anything that might offend the reader.

> **WRITING SPEAK**
>
> Specific, vivid verbs add power to your résumé. Use them to explain both professional and educational experiences.

Example 1

Dena H. Kosinsky
46 Sandhill Road
Morristown, NJ 07960
800-555-1212
dhkosinsky@acmeinternet.com

Objective

To obtain an entry-level position requiring strong organizational and writing skills in the paralegal department.

Education

Eastern Virginia University
B.S. in Paralegal Science, May 2003
Honors: Alumni Prize for Legal Writing, 2003
Phi Beta Kappa

Professional Experience

Intern; Whittlesey, Smith, and Starbuck; Waitsfield, Virginia; Spring 2002
Assisted partner by performing legal research, writing memoranda, and filing pleadings.

Writer; Morristown Daily Citizen; Morristown, New Jersey; Summer 2001 and 2002

Covered court and police activity for community newspaper. Conducted interviews, gathered research, and wrote articles.

Computer Skills

DBASE IV, QBASIC, Word, Excel

Activities and Interests

President; Paralegal Society; campus chapter; Fall 2000–present Tutor; Campus Writing Center; Fall 2001–present

Fluent in Spanish

Example 2

Sam Wildemuth
32 W. Clover Ave., Apt. 3
Redstone, PA 16842
800-555-1212

OBJECTIVE

Hospitality professional with extensive experience, seeks management position.

PROFESSIONAL EXPERIENCE

Banquet/Restaurant/Bar Manager

Radisson Pittsburgh; Pittsburgh, Pennsylvania; 2003–present

Assistant manager of restaurant and catering department that produces over $2 million annually in food and beverage revenues. Duties include menu development, quality and inventory control, product ordering, and cost analysis.

Room Service Manager/Restaurant Supervisor

Redtop Resort; Mountainview, Pennsylvania; 2001–2003

Hired as banquet server and bartender; promoted to Room Service Manager after 6 months. Responsible for staffing, SOP controls and service upgrades. Promoted to Restaurant Supervisor in 2002.

Assistant Weekend Lead Line Cook

Roberto's Trattoria; Holdensville, Pennsylvania; 1998–2001

During college, promoted from part-time server to working in every aspect of food preparation and presentation on weekends.

EDUCATION

B.S. Degree in Hotel/Restaurant Management, 2001

Pennsylvania State College; Holdensville, Pennsylvania

CERTIFICATIONS

TIPS—Health Communications, Inc., 2003

ServSafe—National Restaurant Association Educational Foundation, 2004

EMAIL

Business email is the preferred format for most internal business communications, eclipsing the more formal memo. Its ease of use and immediacy are two of its best features, but they're also two of its biggest detriments. Because it's so quick and easy, many businesspeople feel compelled to send dozens of them each day, relaying information that may or may not be of importance to the recipient(s).

In addition, because emailing is so immediate, it's easy to forget that they have permanence. They're not the same as an offhand remark, or a quick phone call to a friend. Emails are not intimate communications. They can be stored, printed, and even used against you in a court of law. Don't make the mistake of treating them too casually.

Getting It Right

Business email is a fast, easy way to communicate with your colleagues. But it's not without its problems. Here is a list of many of those problems, along with simple solutions.

Problem: Because of the volume of emails most people receive each day, they don't read them all.

Solution: First, send only pertinent information to those people who must read it. If you forward jokes or other useless information, or inform your boss daily about minute details of your projects, your email may languish in inboxes or be deleted without being opened.

Second, always use the subject line. Describe the content of your message as concisely and clearly as possible.

Third, be considerate. Emails longer than one page are difficult to read, because the size of the computer screen limits how much text is visible at one time. In addition, avoid using logos and graphics that take up space on the recipient's computer.

Problem: Emails aren't taken seriously.

Solution: You're at work. Write emails as you would any other business correspondence. Avoid using emoticons, such as smiley faces and winks (☺ and ;–)). Use acronyms only if it is common practice in your workplace. Edit and proofread emails as you would any other type of writing; careless errors detract from the seriousness of your message.

Problem: Emails are read, but rarely get a response.

Solution: Be proactive. Many readers put off responding because they haven't been asked directly to do so. When you start asking for very specific responses, you'll start getting them. "Do you have time to meet with me this week?" should be replaced with "Can we meet in my office Tuesday at 11:00?"

Problem: The intent of emails can easily be misinterpreted.

Solution: Without eye contact or tone of voice, emails rely solely on word choice and mechanics to convey intentions. Review the section in chapter 4 on denotation and connotation; don't use words or phrases whose meaning may be misinterpreted. Even punctuation can send the wrong message; don't use double or triple marks, and limit or refrain from using exclamation marks. All capital letters can appear aggressive or angry; use only for headings in longer emails.

Problem: Business emails can be boring.

Solution: Review the section in chapter 4 on clarity and concision. Don't use meaningless words and phrases, but instead choose high-impact words that express your meaning clearly and succinctly. Don't stray from your subject. If it's a full page long, consider opening with a summary.

> **SHARP WRITING TIP**
>
> Take business emails seriously—they can be stored, printed, and used against you; watch tone, use subject lines, and keep it simple.

Email has spawned a language of its own: acronyms that make using this quick communication tool even quicker. Most are not appropriate for business use, unless deemed acceptable by your company. For an extensive list, check www.netlingo.com.

MEMOS

Memos are internal communications that provide information quickly and concisely to a group of people within a company. Their tone is more formal than emails, and less formal than business letters or reports.

Getting It Right

Memos are made up of three parts: heading, discussion, and conclusion. Each part has a specific purpose. The heading is made up of four or five lines that note who the memo is directed to, who prepared it, others who should receive a copy of the memo (if necessary), the date on which it is distributed, and the subject. Use the subject line to draw attention to the memo and capture your reader's attention by writing something specific and important. "Today's Meeting" is vague. "Attendance Requested at Emergency Budget Meeting" works better.

The discussion begins with a strong, concise thesis statement that expands on the subject identified in the heading. It then explains the major points of the subject, using details and examples to support them. Use formatting tools such as headings, indentations, or bold type to organize information in longer discussions.

The conclusion reiterates the goal and main points. If the purpose of the memo is to persuade others to take action or respond in some other way, the conclusion clearly but politely requests it.

> **REMEMBER THIS!**
>
> Learn your company's memo guidelines and follow them. If the company has none, gather examples of recent memos and study them before writing your first memo on the job.

Example

Meekins, Thurber, Jones, and Associates
Memorandum

To: All Employees

From: Jennifer Preston, Human Services Director

Date: January 15, 2006

Re: New Security Entry System

Due to increased security risks, a new entry system will be installed in our building over the weekend. Please familiarize yourself with the new procedures, and be certain to follow the steps outlined below to obtain an entry card before Monday.

Once the new system is operating, employees will need to slide an entry card through a slot (similar to a credit card machine) located next to the front door. If you have trouble, press the red button beneath the slot to speak with the Security Department.

To obtain your entry card, report to the Security Department during this week with photo identification and a letter from your supervisor confirming employment with Meekins, Thurber, Jones, and Associates.

The new system will be working next Monday morning. Due to a need for increased security, the only way to gain entry to the building is described above.

Why It Works

The memo follows the three-part format, using the company's heading. The introduction explains why the new system is necessary, and how to comply with it. The body of the memo discusses the specific details of the system, both how to use it, and how to get the card needed to access it. The concise (two sentence) conclusion reminds the reader why the system is needed and when it will be functional. The tone of the memo is appropriate, being both formal and instructional.

Simplify your business communications by using plain English. Instead of "the purpose and aim of the aforesaid conference," write "the conference is intended to." Rather than "a response is requested within a period of time not exceeding two weeks," write "please respond within two weeks."

> **FLASHBACK!**
>
> In chapter 4, you learned to avoid buzzwords and jargon. This is especially true in business writing. Hiding (unsuccessfully) behind important-sounding, trendy words is an insecure writer.

BUSINESS LETTERS

Business letters are the standard form of communication between two companies, or between an individual and a company. They are written to convey important information, and to provide a permanent record that the information was sent.

Getting It Right

To write a business letter, follow the procedure outlined in section II. First, decide on a subject, and begin prewriting. Create an outline, and write a draft, keeping your audience in mind. Finally, edit the letter to make it more readable and easier to understand, and to eliminate errors in mechanics and grammar. Remember that business letters are addressed to busy people; state your purpose clearly and concisely, and don't stray from your topic.

There are three formats used for the majority of business letters: block, semi-block, and indented. In **block format,** all entries are set on the left-hand margin. **Semi-block format** moves the date and inside address to the right-hand margin. To create an **indented format,** use either block or semi-block, and indent each paragraph five spaces. These formats may be found as templates in most word processing programs. Remember to determine if your company specifies a business writing format before writing your first letter on the job. All of the formats are printed on letterhead that includes the company's name, address, and other contact information.

Here are a few letter-writing tips to improve your business correspondence:

- State your purpose in the first sentence. Your reader wants to know immediately what the letter is about and why he or she should read it.

- If you are responding to another letter, don't assume your reader will remember it. Identify the letter by subject and date in the subject line or first sentence.

- Help your recipient read your letters quickly and remember the important facts or ideas by keeping paragraphs between three and six lines long. One or two sentence paragraphs also work well.

- Relay bad news in a positive way. Your goal is to maintain or develop positive relationships by remaining friendly and tactful no matter the situation. Avoid negative, harsh words such as *cannot, deny, fail, forbid, impossible, prohibit, refuse*, and restrict.
- Concentrate on your reader's concerns, making him or her the focus. If there are too many "I"s or "me"s, your letter is too self-centered.

Depending on the type of letter you are writing, there are as many as 12 elements in a business letter. Their correct use and placement is essential in making your document look professional. The elements are listed in order as they appear on the page, from top to bottom.

Heading: the sender's address and contact information, also known as a letterhead

Date: the date on which the letter was written; placed at the top of the page, at least two lines below the letterhead

Inside Address: recipient's name, and/or professional title, and address; two lines below the date

Salutation: a personal greeting to your reader; two lines below the inside address.

Subject Line: a short phrase that describes the content of the letter (optional); at least two lines below the salutation

Body: the message of the letter; two lines below the salutation or subject line, single-spaced.

Complimentary Close: end of the letter (e.g.: *Sincerely, Respectfully*, or *Cordially*); two lines below last line of the body.

Signature Block: signature of the person writing the letter below the complimentary close; four lines below the closing signature is typed name (followed by the job title when writing on behalf of a company).

Initials: the person signing the letter (all capital letters), colon, followed by the typist (all lowercase).

Enclosure: indicates that additional paperwork is included in your correspondence; use the word *enclosure,* or *attachment*, two lines below the initials.

Copies: if sending copies of the letter to others, indicate it by using *cc* if one or two people, or *distribution* if more; two lines below last notation.

Continuation Pages: any page after the first page of a document. Put the addressee's name, the date, and the page number at the top left corner of each page, flush left. Do not use letterhead for continuation pages.

Examples

Block: Cover Letter

17 Chestnut Street
Austin, TX 78759
6 June 2006

Raul G. Ramirez
Women's and Children's Hospital
4505 Central Ave.
Austin, TX 78703

Dear Mr. Ramirez:

I am writing in response to your classified ad in the Austin Citizen for Assistant Director of Food Service. My experience and education qualify me to fill this position.

For the past three years, I have been employed in the food service industry, working first for Standard Corporate Catering Services, and then for American International Group. I have experience in purchasing, hiring, training, and management.

I received my Associate Degree in Hotel and Restaurant Management in 2004, and have since completed two courses at Butler Community College that will be applied toward a Bachelors Degree.

Women's and Children's Hospital serves a large, diverse community, has been cited as one of the nation's leading medical centers. I would be proud to work for such an organization, and look forward to the challenges and rewards of running a large food service operation. I look forward to hearing from you to arrange a time when we can discuss my qualifications for this position. You can reach me at (618) 555-0991.

Sincerely,

Alice Smith
Encl.: résumé

> **REMEMBER THIS!**
>
> Cover letters are a specialized form of business letter used to bridge the gap between your résumé and the requirements of the job you're applying for.

You can use any format for a cover letter, but don't forget these basics:

- Customize each letter for the position, company, and potential employer
- Identify the position you're applying for in the first sentence, and mention how you heard about it, especially if it was through a personal referral
- Demonstrate that you understand the job requirements and can exceed their expectations
- Replace generalities with specifics; "I am responsible and hardworking" is meaningless. Try instead "At my previous position, I was promoted from clerk to floor manager after my supervisor recommended me."
- Explain anything on your résumé that may be questioned by the reader, including gaps in employment and reasons for leaving a job
- Show that you have researched the company and are familiar with the position
- Be proactive; ask for an interview, and let them know you expect to hear from them, or say that you will contact them to follow up
- Stand out through your skills and experience; use standard paper, fonts, and format
- At the end of your letter, provide your contact information follow up in a week if you haven't received a response

Semi-Block: Adjustment Letter

Designer Fabric Wholesalers Ltd.
56 Industrial Parkway
Tampa, Florida 66069
(315) 555-6789

March 2, 2006

Carolyn J. Stein
Fab Fabrics, Inc.
1267 Main Street
Manchester, VT 05609

Re: Your February 25 letter regarding incomplete shipment

Dear Ms. Stein:

I received your letter about the incomplete shipment you received from our company and regret the inconvenience our error has caused you.

Your account of the problem indicates that 17 yards of Ivory Damask (inventory #4547) was missing from your order. As you know, it wholesales for $42.00 per yard. You requested that if we do not have the fabric in stock, we should credit your account for $714.00. In fact, we do have the fabric, and I am shipping it this afternoon. You should receive it no later than tomorrow by 5:00 p.m.

Please accept my apologies for this unfortunate oversight. Designer Fabrics Wholesalers prides ourselves on excellent customer service. If you experience any other problems with our company, please let me know personally. Thank you for your business, and I look forward to providing you and your clients with our fine fabrics again in the future.

Sincerely,

David H. Morganthau, President
Designer Fabrics Wholesalers Ltd.

DHM:kp

Indented: Inquiry Letter

(not on letterhead)

Peabody Building Supply
P.O. Box 213
Seattle, Washington 52217
August 17, 2005

Mr. Paul Simington, President
Tri-State Tile
98 West End Avenue
New York, New York 10020
Dear Mr. Simington,

My company is the leading supplier of building materials for construction companies working in our city and in the surrounding suburbs. Recently, our tile source informed us that they were leaving the business after 24 years, and we are therefore seeking to secure another source.

Through my research, I found that your company produces the high quality product our customers demand, at price points they will appreciate. Last year, we sold over 1,800 units of tile, and are looking to increase that amount by approximately 6% this year. New construction is up in our area, and is expected to rise for the next three years.

Peabody is very interested in working with your company to provide quality products to our many loyal customers. I would like to meet with you in the near future to discuss this possibility. You can reach me in my office this week to arrange a time and location. I look forward to hearing from you.

Very truly yours,

Cynthia Peabody, Vice President

CP:ggn

Proposals

The purpose of a proposal is to persuade its audience to take action; the action might be buying your company's services, donating grant money to a worthy cause, or allowing you to launch a new program within your company or department.

The subject of the proposal is an anticipated future occurrence. It begins with a present problem or need, and offers a plan that, if implemented, will solve or fill it. The plan is extensively detailed, explaining how it will be done, when it will be done, how much it will cost, and why those who will implement it are qualified. All of these details work together to logically convince the reader that the proposed solution is the best one.

Getting It Right

Before you begin any prewriting exercises for your proposal, consider the following:

Who is your audience? Are your readers in your field? Do they need any background information to understand your proposal? Is there any technical or other field-specific jargon that should be explained or avoided?

What are the needs of your audience? If you're asking them to take action, do they have the time? If you are asking for funding, is it within their budget? If you are asking them to choose you over the competition, what can you do better to fill their needs? Anticipate any questions or concerns they might have, and answer them within the proposal.

Who is your competition? How do they typically approach similar situations? What can you do differently to set yourself apart? Anticipate their solution, and show why, although it is acceptable, yours is superior.

Proposals are formatted as either memos or reports, depending upon audience and subject matter. Internal proposals that are written in one or two pages, for example, usually take a memo form. External proposals that can exceed dozens of pages take the form of a report, whose structure helps organize the large amount of material.

The content of a proposal also varies depending upon subject matter. Here, we'll explain the parts of a proposal; each part won't be necessary for every proposal. Use this list like a menu, choosing those parts will work best for your purposes.

Heading: informal proposals use a four- or five-line memo heading, while formal proposals use a cover page. Both should include the author, the recipient, the date, and a title.

Letter of Transmittal: if the proposal is sent to another company, there should be a letter addressed to the recipient acknowledging the attachment of the proposal.

Abstract, Introduction, or Executive Summary: see the explanation in this chapter's section on Reports.

Table of Contents: necessary only for longer proposals with many headings and subheadings.

Statement of Problem or Need: explain the problem or need that you wish to solve or fill. The more clearly it is defined, the easier it will be to imagine an effective solution.

Background: what is the history of this problem or need? Who wants it solved or filled, and why?

Objectives and Scope: what will a solution to this problem achieve? Speaking generally, how will you arrive at the solution?

Proposed Solution: what exactly will you do to solve the problem or fill the need you've identified? Present facts using visuals such as charts, graphs, and tables to support your ideas. Those facts should clearly lead to the solution.

Implementation Method: how will you arrive at the solution? Explain the steps needed, and include a schedule including start and finish dates, as well as a list of necessary equipment and materials.

Qualifications: summarize your (or your company's) background and experience. What do you have that the competition doesn't? What strengths and skills do you bring to the job?

Costs: breakdown of the costs of the project, explaining if necessary who is responsible for each cost.

Conclusions and Recommendation: confidently highlight the benefits of the solution for your audience, and encourage action.

End Matter: information that may be of value to the reader, but does not warrant inclusion in the body of the proposal. May include appendices such as letter of reference, résumés, schedules, charts, statistics,

> **SHARP WRITING TIP**
>
> Proposals are sales pitches: they convince the reader of a present problem and detail a plan to remedy it.

Reports

Reports are typically longer than memos, and are written to convey information to an audience that will use it to make decisions. For example, a report analyzing the performance of a stock will be used by potential investors to decide whether to purchase shares.

Getting It Right

Reports should present information so it is concise, easy to understand, and useful. These tips will help you achieve those goals:

- Don't include "padding," whether in the form of unnecessary words and phrases, useless appendices, or information that is not essential to the topic
- Write in the active voice
- Use headings and subheadings to guide your reader to the information he or she is looking for; underlining, italics, and bold type may be used for emphasis
- Include visuals, such as graphs, charts, and tables, to make numbers easy to understand, and to provide interest and variety

> **FLASHBACK!**
>
> In section II, you saw how outlines turn prewriting notes into a writing plan. Remember, the outline is not the end product. Reports should contain explanations, recommendations, and conclusions. Think of them as outlines with depth and substance.

There are between four and six components to a business report, depending upon your topic and your company's report protocol. Here's what they should include, with ideas about how to maximize the value of each part:

The **headline** includes the name of the report, author(s), date, and other necessary identifying information. Some companies prefer a distinct cover page for headline information, while others place this information at the top of the first page.

The **table of contents**, if necessary, includes main headings and page numbers. Subheadings and additional information may be included if the length or complexity of the report warrants them.

The **introduction**, also referred to as *the abstract*, or *executive summary*, states the purpose and goal of the report. It offers highlights of the report without describing its content, and relates context (historical, scientific, etc.) if necessary.

The **body** contains all supporting information for the topic. It relays facts, figures, results, examples, and details. Write the body in short paragraphs that include only the most pertinent information. Don't make your reader hunt for what he or she is looking for.

The **conclusion** may provide a result, recommendation, proposal, or concluding judgment. Some reports include a call to action in the conclusion, which persuades readers to respond in specific ways to the information presented in the report.

End matter contains information that is mentioned in the report, but is not included in its entirety. Examples of such information are a graph of data, another report, and historical context. End matter also includes a reference page in which sources consulted during the preparation of the report are listed.

> **REMEMBER THIS!**
> Use appendices in reports if some of your audience might not be familiar with significant background information.

SUMMARY

You've reviewed the six basic formats of business writing, how to maximize the effectiveness of each, and how to avoid the most common errors.

Your **résumé** is an advertisement written to sell you to a potential employer. In order to get noticed and convince him or her that you are the right person for the job, it needs to look perfect. Content should also be presented to put you in the best light. Which is more impressive—your academic qualifications or professional experiences? Place your strongest assets first.

Email is the preferred format for most internal business communications. Its ease of use and immediacy are two of its best features, but if you're not careful, they can also be two of its biggest detriments. Because email is so quick and easy, many businesspeople feel compelled to send dozens of them each day, relaying information that may or may not be of importance to the recipient(s). Treat email as you would any other business correspondence; keep it relevant and to the point, and use your editing skills to correct any mistakes in spelling, grammar, or mechanics.

A **memo** is an internal correspondence that's longer and more formal than an email. Use memos to clearly and concisely convey information to your company's employees, and when you want a paper copy that can be filed and referred to in the future. Write a memo in three distinct parts: the heading, the discussion, and the conclusion.

Business **letters** are the standard form of communication between two companies, or between an individual and a company. They are written to convey important information, and to provide a permanent record that the information was sent. Use one of the three standard formats on company letterhead, and write in a formal but friendly tone.

Proposals are written attempts to persuade someone to take action. They present and analyze a problem or need, and then clearly and logically explain how it can be solved or filled. Proposals may take the form of a memo or a report, and may be anywhere from a few paragraphs to dozens of pages long.

Reports convey detailed information, such as the results of a study or a summary of a lengthy research process. Because the audience of a report will use it to make decisions, consider its usefulness as you write. In addition, keep a report easy to understand; explanations should be clear and concise, without confusing jargon or buzzwords. Write short paragraphs, and include charts, tables, and/or graphs to present some of your information.

CHAPTER 10

Personal Correspondence

In chapter 8 you studied the basic formats of business communications. In this chapter, we'll look at the correspondence you send from home, including handwritten notes and emails to family and friends, letters to the people and companies who provide you with goods and services, and even letters to elected officials.

Most of these are decidedly less formal than business correspondence, but they do follow some rules and social conventions. It's important to know, for example, why you shouldn't forward emails without first verifying that their content is correct, or why an overly aggressive complaint letter probably won't get you the result you want. Learn how best to create effective personal letters, notes, and emails.

LETTERS

What They Are

Is the personal letter in danger of extinction, threatened by the easier, faster email? Perhaps correspondence with family and friends is going electronic, as more people venture online and begin using email, but there are still many occasions when you will need to write and mail a letter.

Personal letters take many forms. The one you write to an elected official is very different from the one you'd write to a friend. Some require the warmth and individuality of handwriting, while others may be typed. In this section, we'll explain the formatting and styling of personal letters, as well as three common occasions on which to write them.

Getting It Right: Form

Personal, typed letters should be formatted as business letters, most commonly in semi-block style. The letter is typed flush left, except for the return address and the date, which are flush right. If you're using letterhead, the return address is not needed, and just the date appears on the right. Use a high-quality 8 1/2 × 11 inch paper in either white, ivory, or cream. Include a return address on a business-sized envelope. Type the letter using a word processor, and print it cleanly. After signing your letter, fold it neatly into thirds.

Informal letters, such as those thanking a relative for a gift or sharing personal news, require a personal touch. They should be handwritten on an appropriate card or stationery. Include a date in the upper right corner, and use a salutation and complimentary closing as you would in a typed letter.

The preferred salutation for personal letters is *Dear.* Use titles such as *Mr., Mrs., Ms.,* and *Dr.* for people whose name is familiar to you, but whom you either haven't met, or have a formal relationship with. If you are writing to someone whose name and title you don't know, use the greeting *Dear Sir or Madam,* or *To Whom It May Concern.* Appropriate complimentary closes for formal situations include *Sincerely, Yours truly, Regards,* and *Best Wishes.* When writing to a friend or family member, you may wish to close with something more casual and familiar such as *See you soon, Love,* or *Kindest Regards.* A post script (P.S.) can be added to a personal letter, setting an afterthought or additional short message at the bottom of the page.

Sample Format: Personal Typed Letter

Return Address Line 1

Return Address Line 2

Date

Salutation

Body Paragraph 1 _____

_____

_____

_____

Body Paragraph 2 _____

_____

_____

_____

Body Paragraph 3 _____

_____

_____

_____

Complimentary Close
Signature

P.S.

Getting It Right: Substance

Personal letters may be formal or informal. When writing to an acquaintance or someone you don't know, such as an elected official or customer service representative, adopt a more formal tone. You want to be taken seriously, and you can accomplish this by paying attention not only to how your letter looks, but also to how you organize and deliver its content.

Begin by defining your purpose. As you prewrite, answer these questions:

Why are you writing the letter, and what result do you expect by sending it?

What do you need to do to achieve the result (e.g., provide background information, evidence, names of others who are affected)?

> **SHARP WRITING TIP**
>
> Even personal correspondence can benefit from prewriting. Think ahead about purpose and appropriate content, and organize your ideas.

Organize your ideas, keeping your desired result in mind; everything in your letter should work toward attaining it.

As you write your formal letter, introduce your topic in the first paragraph. Decide whether to state or imply the result you want, or wait to bring it up at the end of the letter. If you are building an argument with many facts and points to be made, it might be better to wait until the end of the letter, when the conclusion (your desired result) is obvious.

Adopt a tone that says you're serious. Don't use slang or overly casual words and phrases. Use the active voice, and keep sentences short and to the point. Don't allow your emotions to get in the way.

In the body of your letter, use paragraphs to separate different ideas. Clearly and logically develop your argument. If there is more than one paragraph, each one should focus on a separate aspect of the topic and there should be clear links between paragraphs.

In your final paragraph, leave no doubt about your attitude toward your topic. Ask for what you want in a positive way, without threatening or otherwise getting aggressive. "I expect to receive a full refund" is straightforward and positive. "Give me all of my money back within five days or I will contact my attorney" will put your reader in a defensive position from which he or she may respond aggressively.

Opening Phrases That Get to the Point

Thank you for your letter…

I am grateful to you for…

It was kind of you to…

Many thanks for…

I am delighted to announce that…

I was delighted to hear that…

I am sorry to inform you that…

I am writing to let you know that…

I was sorry to hear that…

Letter of Complaint

When you purchase a defective product, experience a company error, or receive poor service, don't simply swear off the product or company. Most businesses *want* to remedy problems; they know the benefits of repeat business and positive word-of-mouth advertising. By channeling your anger or frustration into a well-written letter of complaint, you're likely to get the results you want, and you might even get more. Many companies routinely send coupons, gift certificates, or free products to help right a wrong.

Checklist

- Act quickly, when the details of your transaction are fresh in your mind as well as the minds of the company or serviceperson. There may be a return policy or guarantee that covers your problem.
- Find out to whom to address your letter. It should only take a phone call to get the correct name and title. Use *To Whom It May Concern* if you must, but be certain it is directed to the proper department if it's going to a large company.
- Explain the situation using the Journalist's Questions prewriting technique from chapter 5 to cover *who, what, where, when, how,* and *why.* If you give only the most pertinent information, you should only need a short paragraph.

- Write in a serious but friendly tone. Angry threats and name calling will make it harder for you to get results.
- Provide tangible evidence to support your claims, including copies of receipts, contracts, warranties, and other documents.
- Explain how you want the situation rectified. Do you want a refund? Credit applied toward your account? A replacement product? Be specific.
- Make a copy of the signed letter for your records.
- Call the person you sent your letter to after one week if you haven't received a reply. Tell them you are following up and want to know the progress being made on your claim.
- When you get results, send another letter thanking the person in charge.

SHARP WRITING TIP

Using aggressive language and threats can make your reader feel defensive and therefore unwilling to help you.

Sample Complaint Letter

7014 Main Street, Apartment 2B
Juneau, Alaska 99802
March 18, 2006

Dear Ms. Jackson,

On January 31, I purchased a set of handmade candles from your store. The tag on the candles read, "Dripless. Burn time 20 hours." Copies of my receipt and the tag are enclosed.

That night, I lit the candles at 7:00 as guests began to arrive at my home. After two hours, one of my guests remarked that she smelled smoke. I walked into the dining room, and saw that both candles had completely burned down to the wooden holders, which were smoldering!

Another guest thought quickly and picked up the candle holders and brought them to the kitchen sink. He doused them with water and the smoke subsided. However, both candleholders are ruined. In addition, my tablecloth has two black singe marks where the holders sat, and the marks did not come out at the cleaners. A copy of the cleaner's receipt is also enclosed.

I expect to be reimbursed for the price of the candles ($11.26), the candle-holders ($38.75), the tablecloth ($61.90), and the cleaning bill ($9.50). In addition, I would advise you to discontinue the sale of these candles. They are not only defective, but also dangerous!

I expect to receive reimbursement totaling $111.41 by March 31. Thank you for your attention to this matter.

Sincerely,

Ginny Ackerman

EMAIL

What It Is

Electronic mail, sent from one computer to another, is faster and easier than writing letters, making phone calls, and sending faxes. Email may be sent to one, one hundred, or hundreds of thousands of people at the same time. It is becoming the preferred method of communication for friends and families, organizations and associations, and business colleagues.

Email is more casual than other written communications, and typically retains an informal tone even when the writer and reader don't know one another. It has a language of its own, filled with acronyms such as IMHO (In My Humble Opinion). Email makes keeping in touch with friends, family, coworkers, and others fast and easy. But for all its informality, email is still guided by rules, often referred to as Netiquette (Internet etiquette).

Getting It Right: Form

The first thing your email readers see in their inbox is the subject line. It tells them, briefly, what they can expect to find when they open it. But many writers leave this line blank, thinking of it as an option rather than an integral part of the email. Consider this: many people receive dozens of emails a day, and don't have time to read them all. They rely on subject lines to help them decide what to open, and what to discard. By writing an accurate, compelling subject line, you increase the odds that your email will be read.

> **SHARP WRITING TIP**
>
> Don't send email with a blank subject line.

There are many different software programs used for composing and reading email. Yours may allow you to personalize your message with colors, boldface, italics, underlining, and a variety of fonts. However, some programs can't handle the formatting, and will translate your message into HTML tags. Instead of **boldface,** for example, your reader will see boldface. It's safer to skip the fancy formatting, which will guarantee that your message will arrive in readable form no matter what software your reader is using.

Email attachments, such as Word® documents, pictures, or spreadsheets, can also cause problems. Because computer viruses are easily spread through attachments, many people won't open them, and some even block email with attachments, so it never appear in their inbox. It's best to ask your recipients in a separate email whether they accept attachments. If they do, ask if they have the software necessary to read the attachment, and even if he or she has room on his or her computer for the attachment (pictures, videos, and other types of files can take up hundreds of megabytes).

If you are sending a Web link, you may also have problems caused by differing software programs. Some programs recognize a Web address as beginning with *www* but many only recognize them as beginning with *http://*. To guarantee that your reader will be able to open the link, use the full address.

The casual nature of email can lull writers into thinking they don't need to follow the basic formatting conventions of written correspondence. For example, salutations and closings are often left out. They shouldn't be! Greet your reader with a standard salutation such as *Dear*, or even with a simple *Hello* or *Hi*. Close your letter with your name, which might not appear anywhere else in the email (if your email address doesn't include your full name, and the "from" line only includes only your address).

Getting It Right: Substance

Emails are usually written quickly, and sent unedited. They therefore tend to be terse and contain misspellings and other errors. Some people write in a kind of shorthand, leaving out articles, pronouns, and other "non-essential" words from their sentences (for example, *I am awaiting your response* becomes *awaiting response*). Meaning can even be conveyed without words, using emoticons such as the smiling face ☺ and wink ;)

These casual hallmarks of emails are accepted by many of its users, especially younger ones who've grown up with email. But not everyone appreciates or even understands them. Acronyms and emoticons, for example, may be a mystery to a new, older emailer. Consider your audience when sending email, and be certain that your message is readable and inoffensive to them.

More Emailing Tips

When sending an email to a number of people who don't know one another, don't enter their email addresses in the "To" field. Many people consider their address to be private information, and do not want it shared with strangers. Instead, address the email to yourself, and enter the addresses in the "Bcc" field (use the "help" feature of your email software for specific instructions). That way, no one will see the list of recipients' email addresses.

Length

Keep it short. Email is read on a screen that only shows about 20 lines at a time. Try to keep emails that length or shorter. In addition, some email software breaks lines longer than 75 characters. While your message may look fine on your screen, your reader may see part of a line, and have to scroll right to read the rest. Some programs even delete characters after a certain number, which would make most emails incomprehensible. By breaking lines at or before the 75-character mark, you assure readability for any email recipient.

Forwarding

Think twice before forwarding emails. With the ease of forwarding, one message can circulate to millions of people in a short period. Many such emails are jokes, with graphics and/or animation that may take time to download and take up valuable space on the recipients' computers. Others fall into the category of "urban legends" or email hoaxes, most of which are false. These include stories about car thieves' techniques, abductions, and product safety warnings. To check the veracity of such an email before forwarding it, search for its title or first line (in quotation marks) on a search engine. Do some research to find out the source of the information, and whether a website such as www.snopes.com, www.urbanlegends.com, or www.scambusters.org has ascertained whether it is true. Don't be guilty of disseminating rumors, lies, or exaggerations.

> **SHARP WRITING TIP**
>
> Don't forward emails without checking first to see if the content is accurate.

If you decide to forward an email, clean it up. The person you're sending it to doesn't need to receive five pages of strangers' addresses and notes to one another. Delete everything in the body of the email except for the message itself. Not only does it show that you value your recipient's time, but it makes the message more readable too.

Tone

The tone of an email can easily be misunderstood because there are no facial expressions, tone of voice, or body language to help convey it. Comments that could be easily misunderstood, such as an ironic *I can't wait to see that one* or *There's nothing I like more*, should be left out.

Adding emphasis to key words can also be tricky. We've already explained how italics and underlining can be unreadable by some email software programs. So how do you add emphasis to a word or phrase? Some writers capitalize entire words, but this is often interpreted as shouting, and it can be hard to read. Try instead placing the word within asterisks; for example, *I already told you I *don't* accept emails with attachments*!

SUMMARY

Personal correspondence can be formal or informal, serious or light-hearted. It can take the form of a letter to a business requesting a refund, or a thank you note to your cousin expressing gratitude for a birthday gift. Personal emails are exchanged with friends, family members and groups such as sports teams, civic organizations, and community organizations. Let's review what we covered in this chapter about how best to approach these types of correspondence.

Some personal **letters** should be typed and formatted as you would a business letter. They are the letters you write when you want to be taken seriously, and desire a result. Examples include letters of complaint and letters requesting information. Other letters should be **handwritten**, because they need to convey a more personal message.

Take care when sending personal emails to ensure that your message arrives in a readable form, and gets the attention of your recipient. Don't send attachments without first asking if they're accepted. Keep your e-mails short to make them easier to read and respond to, and don't clutter up friends' and family's inboxes with hoaxes and "urban legends." Before forwarding any email, check to see if it's true.

CHAPTER 11

Academic Writing

Academic or scholarly writing takes different forms based on the discipline in which you're writing. Engineering students, for example, will be asked to write reports based on designs and laboratory findings. English majors analyze literature and write essays. History students digest information from many sources and use it to develop unique ideas in their papers.

The two major categories, reports and essays, have already been explored at length in this book. You've learned how to prewrite to come up with a plan for writing, how to write a strong thesis statement, and how to use the introduction, body, and conclusion of your writing to great effect. All of these skills are used in academic writing.

This chapter will focus on techniques you'll need to conquer the writing assignments you receive in school, from using style guides to finding and evaluating sources, writing bibliographies, and taking notes.

Audience

One of the most important ways academic writing differs from many other types of writing is its audience: the reader of your report or essay is already at least as well informed on your subject as you are. Your teachers or professors aren't reading to learn something; they're reading to see if *you* learned something. They'll look for:

- proof that you understand your subject
- use of appropriate resources for research
- organization and development of ideas
- clear, intelligent thinking on the subject

Writing for this audience means you won't have to give the kind of detailed background information or context you might in a business report. You can assume that your professor knows who Tennyson or Einstein was; short biographies aren't necessary. Adopt a formal tone that's objective and acknowledges other points of view. Exclamation points, contractions, and ellipses (unless they indicate where cited text has been cut) should be avoided. Don't be rude, harsh, mocking, satirical, or overly critical. Slang and vulgarisms have no place in academic writing. State your case confidently, but without preaching. Review connotation and biased language in chapter 4.

Using Style Guides

Style guides explain how to format your writing, with rules on everything from how big your margins should be to how to create a bibliography. Some disciplines have their own manuals, while others use a general one. Before you prewrite or begin research, find out which style you need to conform to, and get a copy of the manual.

These are the most common style guides, with publishing or Internet access information:

American Anthropological Association Style Guide (anthropology)

http://www.aaanet.org/pubs/style_guide.htm

ACS Style Guide (chemistry)

American Chemical Society; 2nd ed. (1997)

Publication Manual of the American Psychological Association (education, psychology)

American Psychological Association (APA); 5th ed. (2001)

American Sociological Association Style Guide (sociology)

American Sociological Association; 2nd ed. (1998)

Scientific Style and Format: The CBE Manual (biology, medicine, natural sciences)

Cambridge University Press; 6th ed. (1994)

The Chicago Manual of Style (known as "Chicago"; history, philosophy, religious studies, fine arts)

http://www.chicagomanualofstyle.org

Modern Language Association Handbook for Writers of Research Papers (known as "MLA"; English, foreign languages)

Modern Language Association; 6th ed. (2003)

A Manual for Writers of Term Papers, Theses, and Dissertations (known as "Turabian"; used by many undergraduate institutions for all disciplines) University of Chicago Press; 6th revised ed. (1996)

> **SHARP WRITING TIP**
>
> Find out which style guide your school or department follows; purchase a copy for easy reference.

Exam Essays

Writing for an exam, whether it's the SAT, a college final, the GED, or an exit essay, requires excellent time management skills. Before taking the exam, you need to spend time gathering all available information about it and developing a writing strategy. You should walk into the exam knowing exactly what you'll be facing, and how to handle it. You might not be able to eliminate normal test anxiety, but you can take away the fear of the unknown.

How to Prepare

Standardized tests such as the SAT and GED have websites and published study guides that provide critical information such as possible topics, sample essays, and lists of criteria on which your essay will be judged. Take advantage of it all! Try writing on the sample topics, and determine which works best for you. Study the sample essays and figure out how they're structured: What does the introduction look like? Can you find a strong thesis statement? how many paragraphs is the body made up of? How do those paragraphs function? Is there a formal conclusion? are the grammar, punctuation, and spelling perfect?

Practice writing appropriate essays, and time yourself. Compare your essay with the list of criteria your scorer will be looking for. For the GED, they include well-focused main points:

- clear organization
- development of ideas
- appropriate sentence structure and word choice
- correct punctuation, grammar, and spelling

Some state exams will score your prewriting notes and outline. Understand exactly what is required of you, and practice until you can get it right.

Work with the Clock

Every minute counts when taking a timed essay exam. Not only must you develop strong ideas that address the topic, but also you must organize them, write them with a minimum of mechanics errors, and support them with examples and details.

Begin by prewriting, and use the strategy that you chose during practice sessions. If the topic is new to you, spend a minute or two thinking about it. Why is it being asked? Is it looking for facts or opinion? If it can be approached in a number of ways, which way can you best support? Write your ideas in a loose outline form (don't spend time trying to make it perfect). Fill it in with examples and details, but remember you will have time to come up with more during the writing process.

The bulk of your time should be spent writing (in fact, if errors in punctuation, spelling, and grammar won't be held against you, use all but a few final minutes to write). Begin with an introduction that includes a strong thesis statement that refers directly to the topic. You might even include some of the key words used in the topic in your thesis statement. This will reinforce the idea that you understand it, and your essay will address it clearly and deliberately.

The body of your essay is comprised of the main points you will make about your topic. They should be developed and supported by details and examples. In other words, don't rely on unsubstantiated generalizations. "Hemingway was one of the greatest writers of the 20th century" is simply opinion. But if you preface the statement by noting: "Hemingway not only won the Pulitzer and Nobel Prizes for literature, but his four major novels, *The Sun Also Rises* (1926), *A Farewell to Arms* (1929), *For Whom the Bell Tolls* (1940), and *The Old Man and the Sea* (1952), are read and studied as much today as they were 60 years ago" you've substantiated it.

Use paragraphs to organize your essay, and don't stray from your topic. If you decide to use a quote or an important date, and aren't sure if you have it right, qualify it. Instead of hesitatingly noting, "the Civil War started in 1860," write, "the Civil War started in the 1860's," or "the Civil War started in the mid-nineteenth century."

REMEMBER THIS!

Leave room in both your outline and your essay to add information. You might think of a better detail or example as you write, or notice while revising that you could use a better transition between two paragraphs.

In the concluding paragraph, restate your topic and the points you made in the body of your essay. Emphasize the fact that you stayed on topic, and that your points developed it and were well supported. Don't contradict any of your points or introduce new material. You also shouldn't repeat your introduction, or use clichés such as "It just goes to show," or "This essay was about."

When you're finished writing, you should have a few minutes to revise it. If you'll be penalized for errors in spelling, punctuation, and grammar, check for them. As you re-read the essay, make sure you included examples, details, and/or evidence in each paragraph. The tone should be consistent. Expand any confusing sentences or phrases, and eliminate those that don't pertain to your topic.

Here's a sample test response:

QUESTION

There are five elements of literature. Delineate and define each element, and using a popular children's story (i.e., *Little Red Riding Hood*), give an example of each element from the story.

Poor Response:

There are five elements of literature. These include title and author, plot, main characters, setting, and conclusion.

The title, in this case, *Little Red Riding Hood*, tells what the story is about. Sometimes, it can be misleading. The author is the person who wrote the book. In this case, it is a fairy tale and has been around a long time. Thus, it does not really have an author.

The plot tells what happens in the story. In this story, a child is on a journey to her grandmother's house. She stops to talk to a wolf. The wolf then tricks her. The main characters in the book are the little girl, the wolf, and her grandmother.

The setting is another element. The setting where the story takes place. This story takes place in the woods and at grandma's house. The final element is the conclusion. This is the final event that takes place. In this case, the grandmother is saved and everyone is happy.

This essay has some of the elements correct (the elements are plot, characters, setting, theme, and point of view), but others that are incorrect. Although the essay itself does contain correct grammar and spelling, it does not include transitions. In addition, three things were required for each of the elements. Each element was to be named, defined, and illustrated by an example from the story. In order to receive higher points, the writer would need to make sure all six elements were correct and that each of the three parts for each element was included.

Strong Response:

The five elements of literature include plot, characters, setting, theme, and point of view. Each of these elements are present in every story.

The first element is plot. The plot is the action that takes place in a story. In the story, *Little Red Riding Hood*, the main action centers around Little Red Riding Hood. She is walking through the woods to her grandmother's house when she encounters a wolf. She gives the wolf information and then he uses that information to go to her grandmother's house to trick her. In the end, the grandmother and a woodcutter help destroy the wolf.

The second element involves the characters in the story. In this story, the characters are Little Red Riding Hood, the Big Bad Wolf, the grandmother, and the woodcutter. The characters are the main people (or animals) who are involved in the action of the story.

The third element is the setting. This involves the places where the action takes place in the story. In *Little Red Riding Hood*, there are two settings. The first is the woods on the way to the grandmother's house. The second is the grandmother's house.

The fourth element is theme. The theme is the moral of the story. It is the main message the story is trying to convey. In this story, the main idea for children to learn is not to talk to strangers. Because the little girl talks to the wolf, there is trouble later. Children reading this story learn not to talk to strangers.

The final element is point of view. This involves what person the story is written in as well as who is telling the story. This story is written in third person. It is, however, written from the point of view of the main charac-ter—the little girl.

In conclusion, there are five main elements of literature. Each contributes in its own way to the story. The plot, characters, and setting tell us what is happening to whom and where it is taking place. The theme tells us the moral of the story, and the point of view helps us know who is telling us the story.

This essay answers the question fully. It includes the five correct ele-ments (plot, characters, setting, theme, point of view) and it gives the three requirements for each element (name it, define it, and give an example from the story of it). The essay is well written and includes transitions. It follows the format of having an introductory paragraph (telling the main points), a body (explaining the main points), and conclusion (wrapping up the main points).

Research

If your assignment requires research, you must find source material (works written by others) and use it to support your topic. Not only will you con-sult library books, periodicals, and other documents, but you'll also search the Internet for information. Staying focused when there's so much mate-rial at your disposal can be difficult. It's important that your topic is spe-cific before you begin research. Try writing a thesis statement that declares your approach, and put the statement at the top of each page on which you take notes. Don't lose focus.

To begin, study your primary source before embarking on a search for the opinions of others. Understand your source, and consider an original approach if the assignment calls for one. What interests you most about it? How did you initially respond to it? Has that response changed? Some of the prewriting techniques you learned in chapter 5, such as asking the journalists' questions, can help narrow down your topic. Don't start sifting through secondary sources until you have a firm understanding of your approach.

Consult sources in this order:

1. Primary Sources: the text you're writing about, or documents that directly relate to it. If you're writing a paper on Romantic Poetry, the poems themselves are primary sources. If your topic is The Erosion of Civil Liberties, your primary sources will be the Bill of Rights, and any Executive Orders, Laws and Regulations you find applicable.

2. Secondary Sources: what other people have said about your topic. The paper on poetry would probably benefit from a reading of sources providing biographical information, critical analysis, and historical context. The Civil Liberties paper might be enriched with books, articles, and essays that furnish legal background, reasoned opinion, and even public sentiment. Begin with general reference materials, and work toward more specialized ones:

   • Encyclopedia, dictionaries, other reference works (paper texts or online)
   • Library catalogue, sources listed in the first bullet.
   • Sources cited in bibliographies and notes of sources in the second bullet.
   • Periodical indexes that list articles on your subject
   • Websites with content specific to your topic

Taking Notes

Using secondary sources is an integral part of research. However, it can also be dangerous. If you don't cite those sources properly, that is, if you don't acknowledge that you consulted them, you're plagiarizing. If you string many quotes and borrowed ideas together, you've created a catalogue of your sources, not an original paper. While it is not expected that every idea in your paper will be your own, you must give credit when you borrow, and synthesize the information you've gathered with your thinking on your topic. Don't simply restate the words and thoughts of others.

> **SHARP WRITING TIP**
>
> Acknowledge all sources, and cite them properly to avoid plagiarism (check your style guide for help).

The best way to safeguard against plagiarizing is to take great notes during your research. Notes will help you organize the material you've gathered, and eventually create a formal bibliography of works consulted. Some students use sheets of paper for notes, while others prefer index cards. Either way, here are some guidelines for note taking:

- Check your style guide for information needed for the bibliography
- Create a master list of works consulted as you research (see the section later in the chapter on bibliographies)
- Organize notes as you take them; if you're using cards, put only one note on each card, and label it by topic or sub-topic; if you're using pages, label the pages with topics and sub-topics, and list related notes together
- Don't crowd; leave plenty of room for additional thoughts and notes to be added
- Add your comments in another color ink as you respond to information
- Use exact quotes only when a phrase or sentence stands out as truly memorable, one that you may use in its entirety in your writing
- Summarize the most relevant ideas using short phrases and key words (full sentences are not necessary)
- If the source is a borrowed book, consider using post-it notes to add comments and point to important sections of the text
- Remember to include page numbers for each note

Example: Note Card

source: Barrow, <u>Origin of Universe</u>   p. 60
<u>Universe—"everything that is," might be infinite or finite</u>
<u>Visible universe—finite part of universe, increases in size</u>
<u>over time</u>

Practice 1

Create a note card for each of the following passages.

1. Katharine S. White, <u>Onward and Upward in the Garden</u> (New York: Farrar, Straus and Giroux, 1979; Boston: Beacon Press, 2002) page 163. "The first power mower was conceived in Detroit, when a Colonel Edwin George attached the gasoline-powered engine from his washing machine to his lawnmower. It did the trick, and in 1919 he established a company to make and sell his Moto-Mower."

2. Arthur Herman, <u>How the Scots Invented the Modern World</u> (New York: Crown Publishers, 2001; New York: Three Rivers press, 2001) page 345. "The Scottish mass migration of the eighteenth and nineteenth centuries...was as momentous as any in history. In sheer numbers, it hardly stands out; perhaps 3 million all told, compared to the 8 million Italians who left their native land between 1820 and World War I. Yet its impact was far-reaching in more ways than one."

3. Ludlow Griscom, Audubon's Birds of American (New York: The Macmillan Company, 1950) page 16. "In 1831 he made his famous expendition to the Flordia Keys, the next year going to Labrador, then traveling through the southern states to the independent republic of Texas, always seeking out wilderness ares."

4. Carol Shields, Jane Austen (New York: Viking Penguin, 2001) page 75. "It is a cliché to think of Jane Austen's life as being without event, since insanity, treason, illegitimacy, and elopement invaded her quiet family circle, and even, once or twice, criminal proceedings. In 1799 her aunt, Jane Leigh-Perrot, was accused of stealing a piece of lace from a Bath shop. For this presumed crime she was imprisoned for several weeks and tried at Taunton assizes, where she was eventually acquitted."

Evaluating Sources

Remember the cliché, "you can't judge a book by its cover?" It may be trite, but it's solid advice. Just because a book has a glossy cover and a few glowing blurbs on the back proclaiming it to be well received doesn't mean you should trust it. Sources are not all of the same quality. The only way to determine whether you've found something reliable is to do some evaluating. Don't use any source until you have determined that it provides strong, credible support for, and information on, your topic.

Two important criteria to use for evaluating sources are **bias** and **timeliness.** Some books are written by writers who purport to objectively examine a subject when in fact they simply promote an agenda. For example, if you were researching the subject of gun control, would you rely on a book published by the National Rifle Association, which is admittedly against any kind of control? Unless you understand the bias of the publisher, you risk including skewed statistics and other unreliable information.

Many subjects change over time. Scientific research, new rulings, and even shifting public opinion can make information obsolete. If you're writing about the Fourth Amendment and its use by opponents of random drug testing, you need to find the most current information. Courts reverse decisions, legislation is passed, and regulations are approved frequently. Relying on a six-month-old resource when you're dealing with an ever-changing subject such as law is risky.

Internet resources present special challenges to researchers. Websites are easy and relatively inexpensive to create, making it possible for almost anyone to publish information on the Internet. As with books, the mere facts of a website's existence and appearance do not guarantee value. Before relying on any information found on the Internet, you need to evaluate its source.

Legitimate websites have **authority.** At the bottom of most home pages, you can find the contact information for the person, organization, or institution that wrote or is responsible for the content of the site. A full name or names, address, phone number, and email address should be provided. If you can't find the information, shorten the URL (Web address) by deleting everything to the right of first slash (which is commonly preceded by .com, .org, .edu, or .gov). Is a responsible author identified? Don't rely on information from the site unless you can determine who claims responsibility for its content.

Don't stop asking questions once you've found the author of the site. Do you know if the person or groups is qualified to write on the topic? What are his or her credentials? If the author is a group or organization, is it legitimate? Try to find similar information on three other websites that have not copied it from the original site. Look up the author or organization. Do they exist as they say they do? Is the contact information correct?

As with information from books and periodicals, the data you find on the websites could be obsolete. Are there links to other pages? Try them to see if they work; links to pages that no longer exist could mean the site you're looking at hasn't been updated in a while. Internal clues can also date the site. Are there "current" references to old material (for example, is the 1996 presidential election referred to as the most recent)? Check the bottom of the home page for a date on which the site was last revised. If there is no date, or it's been a few months (or longer), question the information. Most legitimate sites are well maintained.

Sites created by individuals often contain the most unreliable information. Individuals do not have to pass any test of accuracy or legitimacy before posting content on their own website. That's not to say that all personal pages are bad sources, but rather that you should evaluate them more carefully. Before you determine the author, credibility, or currency, check the URL for clues. A personal Web page URL typically has one or more of the following: a tilde (~), a percent sign (%), the word "member," or the word "user."

SHARP WRITING TIP

Before relying on information found on the Internet, determine whether the source is reliable.

The Formal Bibliography

During the course of your research, you don't need to consult a style guide every time you refer to a different source. Instead, compile a **working bibliography** that contains all of the information you'll need to later style a formal one. Study the citation examples in the guide you'll be following, noting the kind of information required (typically, author's name, title of work, publisher, place and date of publication, and exact quotes with page numbers). If you're using the Internet for research, learn how to write electronic citations.

Many researchers prefer to use **note cards** for keeping track of bibliographical information. Beginning in the upper-left-hand corner, place the author's name and title of the work. Then list the place and date of publication, the publisher, pages consulted, and any other pertinent information, such as date of the edition, number in a series, and volume and edition number of periodicals. Other essential data includes the library and call number, URL, and other source identification so you can easily relocate the material if necessary.

Your style guide will determine the formatting of your formal bibliography. For example, MLA dictates that a book by one author should be cited with author's last name first, followed by the first name and a period. APA uses just the initial of the author's first name. Type carefully, following all rules for spacing, indentation, punctuation, alphabetization, and composition of individual citations. Remember to list every work you consulted, and not just those quoted directly in your work.

SUMMARY

Instead of revisiting the subjects of essays and reports, including how to write an effective conclusion, and why to use appendices in reports, we focused in this chapter on the specific skills you need to write well in an academic setting.

Audience

Scholarly writing is read by a unique audience, one that is as well informed as, or perhaps better informed on your subject than you are. That means the focus is as much on you as it is on your topic. You need to show that you have learned something about your topic, and that you developed and organized ideas about it.

Style

Style guides are used by most institutions to achieve conformity in student writing. The guides dictate how to format essays and reports, how to style footnotes and endnotes, and even how to punctuate. Some disciplines have their own style manuals, and others use more general ones such as MLA, Chicago, and Turabian. Don't turn in a writing assignment without first finding out which guide you need to follow, and then using it to create your finished product.

Preparation

Before you take an essay exam, **prepare thoroughly.** If possible, get information about the test online, or from a published study guide. If it's an exam for a class, study your notes. Practice prewriting and writing essays while the clock is ticking. The better prepared you are, the easier it will be to write a well-crafted essay.

Reference

Don't consult secondary research sources until you have a good understanding of your topic and its primary sources. Begin with reference books and Internet sources of general information. Then, move on to more specific books, articles, and websites. Take notes for each source you consult, and cite the details you'll need to create a formal bibliography.

Before relying on a source, determine its credibility. Print and Internet information should be questioned for authorship (including credentials), bias, and currency. Pay particular attention to personal Web pages, which are notoriously inaccurate.

During your research, create a working bibliography that contains relevant details about each source you consult, such as author's name, title of work, publisher, date and place of publication, and pages read. When you're finished writing, translate the working bibliography into a formal one. Use your style guide, which will determine alphabetization, spacing, and indentation, as well as individual citations.

PRACTICE ANSWERS AND EXPLANATIONS

Cards will vary, but should contain the author's name, title (may be condensed), and page number. Content should be a brief summary, using phrases and key words. If copying text word-for-word, it must be in quotation marks.

Practice 1

1.

source: White, <u>Onward Upward</u>	p. 163
first power mower made by Colonel Edwin George, Detroit	
gas-powered washing machine engine attached to lawnmower	
1919 started company to make, sell Moto-Mower	

2.

source: Herman, <u>Scots Invented Modern Word</u>　　　p. 345
<u>Scottish mass migration 18th–19th centuries</u>
<u>Lower number than other countries: 3 million to</u>
<u>Italy's 8 million</u>
<u>But had "far-reaching" impact</u>

3.

source: Griscom, <u>Audubon's Birds</u>　　　p. 16
<u>travels through wilderness:</u>
<u>1831 went to Florida Keys</u>
<u>1832: labrador, southern states, republic of texas</u>

4.

source: Shields, <u>Jane Austen</u>	p. 75

Austen's life not uneventful as many believe
Family experienced insanity, treason, illegitimacy, elopement, and run-ins with the law
Aunt Jane Leigh-Perrot accused of shoplifting in 1799
She was imprisoned, tried, and acquitted

Sharp Writing Cumulative Test

Congratulations on completing all the chapters and their exercises. Now challenge yourself by answering the following question sets and on your own paper try your hand at several writing exercises. The question sets focus first on some of the very basic elements of writing and the more common errors, and then on your editing and revising skills.

If you get any answers wrong, or find yourself uncertain about how to approach any of the writing prompts, review the relevant chapters once more.

Part 1

Read each sentence below carefully. Determine what part of speech is needed to fill in the blank.

1. Constance walked _____ across the room.

2. I wanted to tell you earlier, _____ I was afraid you'd be angry.

3. That was such a _____ movie!

4. Please give me _____ coat.

5. Did you see that _____?

Part 2

Match each of the following terms to its example (we've done the first for you).

Term	Choice	Example
6. independent clause	b	a. I was waiting for the bus, it never came.
7. fragment, phrase		b. I was waiting for the bus.
8. run-on, comma splice		c. and, or, nor, for, so, but, yet
9. coordinating conjunction		d. Waiting for the bus
10. subordinating conjunction		e. since, because, after, although

Part 3

Correct any pronoun errors in the following sentences.

11. Either Paul or Rita will bring their video camera.

12. On the news they said that the president will be in town tomorrow.

13. A good doctor listens to his patients' words as well as their bodies.

14. To who should I address this letter?

15. If you talk to Rajesh before me, tell him I need my notebook back.

Part 4

Match each of the following terms with its example. We've done the first one to get you started.

Subject	Predicate
Linking verb	Indirect object

16. <u>Scientists</u> know very little about the African bush elephant.
17. I am studying <u>the African bush elephant</u>.
18. <u>Because they live so deep in the jungle</u>, no one knows for sure how many bush elephants there are.
19. The African Conservation Society has given <u>me</u> a grant for my research.

Unscramble the following choices separately.		
20. Simple sentence		A. Because they live so deep in the jungle, no one knows for sure how many bush elephants there are; I intend to find out.
21. Compound sentence		B. Because they live so deep in the jungle, no one knows for sure how many bush elephants there are.
22. Complex sentence		C. I am a research scientist.
23. Compound-complex sentence		D. I am studying the African bush elephant, and I have received a grant for my research.

Part 5

Correct any sentence structure errors in the following paragraph.

According to many experts. Most Americans do not get enough sleep. While adults can often function on just a few hours of slumber. Children and teenagers should get nine to ten hours of sleep each night, otherwise their health and schoolwork will suffer. Studies show that nearly one-third of school-age children. Do not get enough sleep. Many parents don't recognize that their children are sleep deprived, these tired children actually are overactive during the day. Instead of sleepy. Tired children are more likely to have accidents, they have less effective memories and shorter attention spans. It may be difficult to get children to bed earlier however it is clearly very important. That they get enough rest.

Part 6

For each of the following verbs, identify the form or tense indicated.

	look	sleep	ride	do	be
base					
present participle					
past participle					
3rd person singular simple present					
simple past					
past perfect					
future perfect					

Part 7

Circle the correct alternative to complete each of the following sentences.

24. I didn't think it was possible, but Kendra (may / could) win this debate after all.

25. Global warming (could be / could been) *the* main issue in the next election.

26. I do not (care / caring) about the cost.

27. With the (raising / rising) cost of (raising / rising) cattle, many small farms have gone out of business.

28. Some diseases can (lay / lie) dormant in a patient for years before the patient becomes symptomatic.

Part 8

Word Sets:

Which word means:

29. to take or receive: _____

    (a) accept   (b) except

30. fully and clearly expressed or defined: _____

    (a) explicit   (b) implicit

31. to convince or guarantee: _____

    (a) assure   (b) ensure   (c) insure

32. location: _____

    (a) cite   (b) sight   (c) site

33. to recommend what should be done: _____

    (a) advice   (b) advise

Which word...

34. ...is a possessive pronoun?

    (A) their

    (B) there

    (C) they're

35. ...is used for comparisons?

    (A) then

    (B) than

36. ...means *to agree*?

    (A) ascent

    (B) assent

37. ...is the verb meaning *to have an impact on*?

    (A) affect

    (B) effect

38. ...should be used with quantities that can be counted?

    (A) amount

    (B) number

Part 9

The following paragraph is a draft cover letter for a résumé in response to a newspaper advertisement. Rewrite the letter to eliminate any inappropriate language and maintain a consistent and appropriate level of formality.

Dear Sir/Madam:

As I perused the newspaper yesterday, I took note of the advertisement for the procurement of a position within your organization.

The job sounds just divine! I'd love to have it. Here's my résumé. You'll see I bring a lot to the table. I'm especially good at number-crunching and tasks of an analytical nature.

Every employer seeks the perfect man for the position. When you check out my résumé, you'll see that I'm the one for you.

I thank you sincerely for your consideration. Can't wait to hear from you!

Part 10

Read the following paragraphs carefully and correct any errors in punctuation.

The playwright Arthur Miller (he was also a master carpenter)

died on Feb. 11 2005, leaving behind a remarkable body of work.

His most famous play is of course Death of a Salesman [1948].

The plays main character Willy Loman (portrayed by Lee J. Cobb

in the original production) is a traveling salesman who believes

success is simply a matter of being liked! Lomans tragedy is so

powerful because it is also so hopeful. Indeed, Miller believed

tragedy "brings us knowledge … pertaining to the right way of

living in the world". Death of a Salesman won the Pulitzer Prize

(in 1951) and has since come to be regarded as the quintessential

American play. In the late 1980's, Miller published his

autobiography and worried that American theater "…was gasping

and near death…" Many critics wondered if Miller was right? The

verdict may still be out, but this much is certain, Miller's plays

remain full of life and lessons for the living.

Part 11
39. List the two uses of a semicolon.

40. List the three main uses of a colon.

41. Explain the function of the dash.

42. List the three main uses of quotation marks.

Part 12
Correct any errors in commas, semicolons, colons, dashes, and quotation marks in the following sentences.

43. "I know one thing for sure", Juliette said; and that is: I'll always love you."

44. Edward Bulwer-Lytton once wrote; But is a word that cools many a warm impulse stifles many a kindly thought puts a dead stop to many a brotherly deed.

45. There are certain principles to which we hold, the sanctity of treaties, good faith between nations, and the interdependence of

peoples from which no country, however powerful, can altogether escape. —*Anthony Eden*

46. There are two things to aim at in life; first—to get what you want—and after that—to enjoy it. —*Logan Pearsall Smith*

47. Money is like love, it kills slowly and painfully the one who withholds it; and it enlivens the other who turns it upon his fellow man. —*Kahlil Gibran*

Part 13

Identify which punctuation mark serves each purpose listed below.

question mark	48. after a direct question
exclamation point	49. to separate two paired words
parentheses	50. to indicate a word or words have been omitted from a quotation
ellipsis	51. after an emotional statement
slash	52. around supplemental information

Part 14

Each of the sentences that follow contains at least one error in spelling, capitalization, and/or italics. Find and correct those errors using standard proofreader's marks.

53. Dustin has submited his Poem *Evening Moods* to a Poetry Contest in Images magazine.

54. This has been a long-trying semester for me, and I am really looking forward to Summer Vacation.

55. Are you refering to the time I said No one compares to Elvis?

56. My brother, professor Elmont, is world-famous for his acheivements in neurosceince.

57. Francisco is my mejor amigo—my BEST FRIEND in the whole World.

WRITING PROMPTS

These prompts are designed to help you practice the skills you acquired from *Sharp Writing*: *Building Better Writing Skills*. Although they each require a different type of writing, and not all might pertain to your situation, we encourage you to complete each one.

Prompt 1

Write a letter soliciting a donation from a business for your charitable organization. You may need to do some research to provide information about the organization, and create an outline that helps organize your ideas. A tone appropriate to your audience should be conveyed through the formatting of the letter, word choice, and level of formality.

Prompt 2

All of the salespeople in your office will be required to attend a training seminar. Write a memo or email to tell them about this upcoming event. Both formats should include a specific, attention-getting subject line, a mention of the fact that attendance is mandatory, and the time, date, and place of the seminar.

Prompt 3

You researched the timed essay exam you'll be taking in three weeks, and found that you will need to develop a point of view on a topic, substantiating it with concrete examples and details. Using the topic and assignment that follow, prewrite in no more than five minutes, creating a list or loose outline of your ideas.

Topic: In one of Robert Frost's most famous poems, the speaker remembers being confronted with two paths in the woods, and choosing the one that is slightly less-travelled. He remarks "with a sigh" that his choice affected the rest of his life.

Assignment: Some people play it safe, taking the well-travelled path, while others deliberately take a different direction. What might be the positive results of the latter? Plan an essay in which you develop your point of view on this issue. Use concrete examples and details from your reading, studies, experiences, and/or observations to support it.

CUMULATIVE TEST ANSWERS AND EXPLANATIONS

Part 1

1. Adverb. The word here would tell us how Constance walked (*slowly, hesitantly, noisily*).

2. Conjunction. A coordinating conjunction—specifically, *but*—would connect these two independent clauses and show the relationship between them. (*However*, a conjunctive adverb, would work only if the two clauses were separated by a semicolon or period.)

3. Adjective. The word here would tell us what kind of movie it was (*fantastic, lousy, remarkable, banal*).

4. Pronoun or possessive. A possessive pronoun (*your, her*) or demonstrative pronoun (*that*) would correctly fill the blank. You could also insert a possessive noun (*John's, the lady's, Eloise's*).

5. Noun. A person, place, or thing would complete this sentence (*man, accident, house, price tag*).

Part 2

6. *b*

7. *d*

8. *a*

9. *c*

10. *f*

Part 3

11. Either Paul or Rita will bring <u>a</u> video camera. (The two singular antecedents are connected by *or* and one is male, the other female. The sentence needs to be revised because no pronoun can agree.)

12. <u>The newscaster</u> said that the president will be in town tomorrow. (The indefinite <u>they</u> should be replaced by a specific noun.)

CUMULATIVE TEST ANSWERS AND EXPLANATIONS *(cont'd)*

13. Good doctors listen to <u>their</u> patients' words as well as their bodies. (The singular generic noun *a good doctor* needs pronouns that include both genders. Instead of using *his or her,* we revised to make the noun plural.)

14. To <u>whom</u> should I address this letter? (*Whom* is the object of the preposition *to,* so it must be in the objective case.)

15. If you talk to Rajesh before <u>I</u> [do], tell him I need my notebook back. (The context makes it clear that the speaker doesn't mean "If you speak to Rajesh before [you speak to] me." The subjective case is required here for the unstated verb *do*.)

Part 4

16. Subject

17. Predicate

18. Indirect object

19. Linking verb

20. (C)   21. (D)   22. (B)   23. (A)

Part 5

In (A) below, fragments are underlined and run-ons are bracketed. In (B), we offer one version of the corrected paragraph. Revised paragraphs may vary as there are many ways to correct these problems.

(A) <u>According to many experts</u>. Most Americans do not get enough sleep. <u>While adults can often function on just a few hours of slumber</u>. [Children and teenagers should get nine to ten hours of sleep each night, otherwise their health and schoolwork will suffer.] <u>Studies show that nearly one-third of school-age children</u>. <u>Do not get enough sleep</u>. [Many parents don't recognize that their children are sleep deprived, these tired children actually are overactive during the day.] <u>Instead of sleepy</u>. [Tired children are more likely to have accidents, they have less effective memories and shorter attention spans.] [It may be difficult to get children to bed earlier however it is clearly very important.] <u>That they get enough rest</u>.

(B) According to many <u>experts, most</u> [*attach fragment*] Americans do not get enough sleep. While adults can often function on just a few hours of <u>slumber, children</u> [*attach fragment*] and teenagers should get nine to ten

CUMULATIVE TEST ANSWERS AND EXPLANATIONS *(cont'd)*

hours of sleep each <u>night.</u> [*separate clauses with a period*] Otherwise, their health and schoolwork will suffer. Studies show that nearly one-third of school-age <u>children do</u> [*connect fragments*] not get enough sleep. Many parents don't recognize that their children are sleep deprived <u>because</u> [*turn independent clause into subordinate clause*] these tired children actually are overactive during the <u>day instead</u> [*attach fragment*] of sleepy. Tired children are more likely to have <u>accidents, and</u> [*separate clauses with comma and coordinating conjunction*] they have less effective memories and shorter attention spans. It may be difficult to get children to bed <u>earlier, but</u> [*separate clauses with comma and coordinating conjunction (or keep* however *and use semicolon*] it is clearly very <u>important that</u> [*attach fragment*] they get enough rest.

Part 6

	look	**sleep**	**ride**	**do**	**be**
base	look	sleep	ride	do	be
present participle	looking	sleeping	riding	doing	being
past participle	looked	slept	ridden	done	been
3rd person singular simple present	looks	sleeps	rides	does	is
simple past	looked	slept	rode	did	was/were
past perfect	had looked	had slept	had ridden	had done	had been
future perfect	will have looked	will have slept	will have ridden	will have done	will have been

Part 7

24. *May. May* means possibility, which is suggested by the context.

25. *Could be.* The modal *could* must be followed by *be.*

26. *Care.* Forms of *do* must also be followed by the base form.

27. *Rising, raising. Rise* is intransitive—it is the *cost* that is *rising. Raise* is transitive and takes the object *cattle.*

28. *Lie. Lie* is intransitive; the diseases *lie.* There is no object.

CUMULATIVE TEST ANSWERS AND EXPLANATIONS *(cont'd)*

Part 8

29. accept

30. explicit

31. assure

32. site

33. advise

34. A

35. B

36. B

37. A

38. B

Part 9

Answers will vary. There are many problems with this letter. The first paragraph is pretentious; the second, too informal, and it contains several instances of slang and jargon (*bring a lot to the table, number crunching*) as well as a pretentious phrase at the end (*tasks of an analytical nature*). The third paragraph is also too informal (*I'm the one for you*), and it also contains sexist language (*perfect man*). The first sentence in the last paragraph is acceptable though perhaps a bit too formal (or at least wordy), while the last sentence is far too casual.

Here is one possible revision, with a consistently formal (but not stuffy) level of formality. (Note also that it is much more concise—pretentious language in particular tends to be wordy—and that we've added a few specific details, such as the job title and name of the newspaper.)

Dear Sir/Madam:

I noticed your advertisement for a data analyst in yesterday's *New York Times*. I am very interested in the position.

CUMULATIVE TEST ANSWERS AND EXPLANATIONS *(cont'd)*

I have several years of experience in accounting and am an excellent problem solver. I believe I have much to offer to your organization.

I have enclosed my résumé for your review. Thank you for your consideration. I look forward to hearing from you.

Sincerely,

Part 10

The playwright Arthur Miller (he was also a master carpenter) died on February 11, 2005, leaving behind a remarkable body of work. His most famous play is, of course, *Death of a Salesman* (1948). The play's main character, Willy Loman (portrayed by Lee J. Cobb in the original production), is a traveling salesman who believes success is simply a matter of being liked. Loman's tragedy is so powerful because it is also so hopeful. Indeed, Miller believed tragedy "brings us knowledge ... pertaining to the right way of living in the world." *Death of a Salesman* won the Pulitzer Prize (in 1951) and has since come to be regarded as the quintessential American play.

In the late 1980s, Miller published his autobiography and worried that American theater "was gasping and near death." Many critics wondered if Miller was right. The verdict may still be out, but this much is certain: Miller's plays remain full of life and lessons for the living.

Corrections to Paragraph 1: The information in the first parentheses is irrelevant and should be deleted. *Feb.* should be written out, and a comma is needed between the day and year. Commas are also needed to set off *of course* and *Willy Loman* and the parenthetical material that follows (the use of parentheses here is fine). The brackets around the date *1948* should be parentheses. *Plays* needs an apostrophe to show possession as does *Lomans*. The ellipsis in the quotation is correct, but the period at the end of the quotation should be inside the quotation marks. The parentheses around *in 1951* should be deleted.

Corrections to Paragraph 2: The apostrophe after *1980* should be deleted; form the plural only with an *–s*. The ellipses at the beginning and end of the quotation should be deleted. *Many critics...right* is a statement, not a question, so the sentence should end in a period. The comma after *certain* should be a colon as the rest of the sentence explains what is certain.

CUMULATIVE TEST ANSWERS AND EXPLANATIONS *(cont'd)*

Part 11

39. Use a semicolon (a) to separate (yet connect) two independent clauses that are closely related and (b) between items in a series when one or more of those items has a comma.

40. Use a colon (a) to introduce quotations, (b) to introduce lists, and (c) to introduce summaries or explanations.

41. Use a dash to set off a word, phrase, or clause for emphasis.

42. Use quotation marks (a) to set off direct quotations, (b) around titles of short works or portions of long works, and (c) around words being used as words.

Part 12

43. "I know one thing for sure," Juliette said, "and that is I'll always love you." [Put the first comma inside the quotation marks; change the semicolon after *said* to a comma, put quotation marks before *and that...*to indicate that the quotation is continued, and eliminate the colon after *is*.]

44. Edward Bulwer-Lytton once wrote, "'But' is a word that cools many a warm impulse, stifles many a kindly thought, puts a dead stop to many a brotherly deed." [Change the semicolon introducing the quotation to a comma or colon (both are correct), put quotation marks around the direct quotation (*But...deed*), enclose *but* in single quotation marks, and insert commas between the items in the list.]

45. There are certain principles to which we hold: the sanctity of treaties; good faith between nations; and the interdependence of peoples from which no country, however powerful, can altogether escape. [Use a colon after *hold* to introduce the list of principles and put semicolons between the items in the list, since the last item contains a comma.]

46. There are two things to aim at in life: first, to get what you want, and after that, to enjoy it. [Use a colon after *life* to introduce the explanation (what those two things are). Insert commas after the introductory words *first* and *after that* as well as after *want*.

47. Money is like love: it kills slowly and painfully the one who withholds it, and it enlivens the other who turns it upon his fellow man. [Use a colon to

CUMULATIVE TEST ANSWERS AND EXPLANATIONS *(cont'd)*

introduce the explanation of how money is like love. Change the semicolon between the two independent clauses connected by the coordinating conjunction *and* to a comma.]

Part 13

48. question mark

49. slash

50. ellipsis

51. exclamation point

52. parentheses

Part 14

All corrections are underlined in the sentences below.

53. Dustin has submitted his poem "Evening Moods" to a poetry contest in *Images* magazine.

54. This has been a long, trying semester for me, and I am really looking forward to summer vacation.

55. Are you referring to the time I said no one compares to Elvis?

56. My brother, Professor Elmont, is world_famous for his achievements in neuroscience.

57. Francisco is my *mejor amigo*—my best friend in the whole world.

CUMULATIVE TEST ANSWERS AND EXPLANATIONS *(cont'd)*

Sample Responses to Writing Prompts

Compare your responses to the examples we provide below.

Prompt 1

Sample 1:

Jane Johnson
Patient Volunteer
Arnold-St. Bernadette Hospital Center
3000 Broadway
St. Louis, Missouri 00007

Ms Alice Jones
Community Outreach Director
Trademark Cards, Inc.
235 Willowy Drive
St. Louis, Missouri 00009

April 19, 2005

Dear Ms Jones:

As a volunteer for the Arnold-St. Bernadette Hospital Center, I am very aware of the generosity of the Trademark Card Company to hospitals in the greater St. Louis area. I am writing to request a donation of greeting cards for use by our Patient Relations department. I'd like to tell you why I believe this donation would be particularly important and helpful to the patients we serve.

The Patient Relations staff greets all patients in the hospital upon arrival. In addition to being sick, patients newly admitted to a large, busy hospital are often frightened, lonely, and overwhelmed by the new environment. Our staff would write personal messages to all the newly admitted people on your beautiful cards and include a phone number of a Patient Relations

CUMULATIVE TEST ANSWERS AND EXPLANATIONS *(cont'd)*

staff member that could answer their questions and help to orient them to their surroundings. Your cards, well known to our patients as messages and love and caring, would provide a warm welcome to people who need it, especially the many children we serve.

Billy is one patient at our hospital. He is six years old, one of five children, and his mother cannot visit him often. While he may not be able to read the message in a Trademark card, he can see the bright colors and know that he is a special because he has received it. Irina, 82 and preparing for heart surgery, could look at the card and know she was not alone and that a volunteer was available to talk to her.

It is for patients like these that I hope you can donate 10,000 cards. I will write frequently to let you know the good results of your generosity. This gift really can make a difference to people who need comfort and reassurance. Please contact me if I can provide you with any additional information. Thank you for your consideration.

Sincerely,

Jane Johnson

Prompt 2

Sample 1:

YOU MUST ATTEND THIS TRAINING (YOU'LL BE GLAD YOU DID!)

There will be a mandatory sales training seminar this Thursday, September 18 at 4:00 in the Blue Conference Room. The seminar is called "Closing Tips from Top Salespeople" and will feature speakers from leading businesses. Signed copies of Ronald Stump's *The Art of Closing Sales* will be on sale. All sales personnel will be expected to attend and arrive promptly. Refreshments will be served.

Prompt 3

Writing plans will vary in form and detail, depending on whether you are writing a timed essay (for which a quick, short plan is needed), a report that will go out in a few hours, or a long term paper or report.

CUMULATIVE TEST ANSWERS AND EXPLANATIONS *(cont'd)*

Sample 1: Free writing

The less traveled road can lead to unusual, life-changing experiences, one you wouldn't have thought of except for this path.

Think of Mom's decision to move to Vermont after her divorce. Took guts for a woman with two small kids to pick up stakes and move to another state. It certainly wasn't what people advised her to do

We city kids had never seen that much green or wildlife. We learned to enjoy finding and exploring hidden trails and usually saw the most interesting birds and flowers there.

Mom became a park ranger after being a secretary all her life. I plan to study botany.

It would have been easy to stay, but she took a path that helped us all grow.

Sample 2: Outline

   I. Introduction
      A. Nothing ventured, nothing gained.
      B. The path less traveled offers the possibility for the unexpected. Taking a chance on the unknown can open new possibilities.
      C. My father took a different path from his five brothers and he has been very successful and happy in his work.

  II. Working-class boys in England during the 1950s generally left school at fourteen and learned a trade. My father wanted to continue on in school and get a college education.
      A. The difficulty of making an unusual choice. Resisting expectations of class and background
      B. Lack of support from family because following a different path. Because my father's path was different, it was strange and threatening to his parents.
      C. Necessary to be independent and confident in one's choice.

CUMULATIVE TEST ANSWERS AND EXPLANATIONS *(cont'd)*

III. Positive gains from taking the path less traveled

    A. Following one's own course, fosters independence and self-confidence.

    B. Travel to places and learn things. For example, my father went to college in London, earned his doctorate in physics and moved to America to be an astronomer.

    C. His brothers became bricklayers, a more traditional path. They have also been successful at their trade, but this would not have been right for my father.

    D. Most people who take the road less traveled do so because they are pursuing something that interests them. Following your dream brings it own rewards.

IV. Conclusion

    A. The path less traveled is so for a reason; it is either harder to travel or longer.

    B. Taking this path requires strength and conviction. Because these qualities are usually found in people who choose to take the more challenging or difficult way, this path often leads to success.

    C. There is something exciting about striking out where few other people have been. My father has followed a path almost totally unique for someone of his background and certainly so within his family. There is a certain loneliness to the path he chose, but he also takes pride in having defied people's expectations and his work is a source of great pride and enjoyment.

Notes

Notes

Notes

Notes

Notes

Notes

Notes